PROGRAMMING FOR PROBLEM SOLVING USING C

AS PER JNTU-KAKINADA SYLLABUS

T N S KOTI MANI KUMAR

Contents

Preface *v*

Acknowledgements *vii*

1. Introduction To Computers 1

2. Operators, Making Decisions & Repetition 71

3. Arrays,strings, Structure And Unions 159

4. Pointers 223

5. Functions And Files 257

About The Author 311

PREFACE

This book introduces basic concepts of C-Programming, and it is simple and easy to understand for beginners. This book is made up of a large number of programs with clear and easy explanations and also contains tables and diagrams whenever necessary.

This book is useful for students to prepare for competitive exams like University exams, code-vita, hacker rank, etc. This book helps to give more information for B.E/B. Tech, M.E/M.Tech (CSE, IT), M.C.A, B.sc (Computer Science) M.sc (Computer Science) students of various universities in India.

The **1st chapter** gives detailed information about the Introduction, features of C-Programming, identifiers, data types, variables, implicit and explicit conversions.

The **2nd chapter** helps you to understand selection and making decisions like if, if-else, if-else ladder, nested if, switch statements, loops or repetition for loop, while loop, do-while loop, jump statement. and operators.

The **3rd chapter** helps you to understand 1-D, 2-D arrays, string handling functions, the array of strings, and structures and unions.

The **4th chapter** helps you to understand pointers and the dynamic memory allocation concept.

The **5th chapter** deals with functions, recursion, and files.

T. N. S. Koti Mani Kumar B.Tech, M.Tech, (Ph. D)

ACKNOWLEDGEMENTS

I would like to thank the following people without whom I would not have been able to complete this great achievement and without whom I would not complete this book.

#include <stdio.h>

void main()

{

printf("I would like to thank the **Managementof Sir C R Reddy College of Engineering** for encouraging and supporting constantly to write this book\n");

printf("Special thanks to **Dr.K. Venkateshwararao,** **M.Tech,Ph.D,** Principal of Sir C R Reddy College of Engineering, Eluru\n");

printf("I would like to extend my deep gratitude to **Dr.A.Yesu Babu,** **M.Tech, Ph.D.,** professor and head of CSE, Sir C R Reddy College of Engineering\n");

printf("I would like to thank especially **Dr.M.Krishna,** **M.Tech, Ph.D.,** professor in CSE, Sir C R Reddy College of Engineering\n");

printf("My sincere thanks to all the **staff members of the CSE Department** of Sir C R Reddy College of Engineering for their generous attitude and friendly behaviour\n");

printf("I would like to thank **M.Harsha Jayanth, M.Tarun Sandeep, P.Sathwik Ram, N. Praveen Kumar, B. Sudheer Babu and Ch. Siva Satyam** for carefully composing the book");

}

Last but not least a word of gratitude to my loving parents and family members for raising me to believe in myself that everything possible and who is always there is giving me support and encouragement.

T. N. S. Koti Mani Kumar **B.Tech, M.Tech, (Ph. D)**

I

INTRODUCTION TO COMPUTERS

CONTENTS: Introduction to Computers, Creating and running Programs, Computer Numbering System, Storing Integers, Storing Real Numbers Introduction to the C Language: Translators, Identifiers, Types, Variable, Constants, Input/output, Scope, Storage Classes, andType Qualifiers. Structure of a C Program, Expressions Precedence and Associativity,Type Conversion Statements, Command Line Arguments.

1. INTRODUCTION TO COMPUTERS :

> *"The computer is an electronic device that takes input from input devices and processes the data and gives output through output devices."*

The computer is a system made up of two major components.

1. **Hardware:** Hardware is a physical component or part of a computer.
2. **Software:** Group of programs is called software

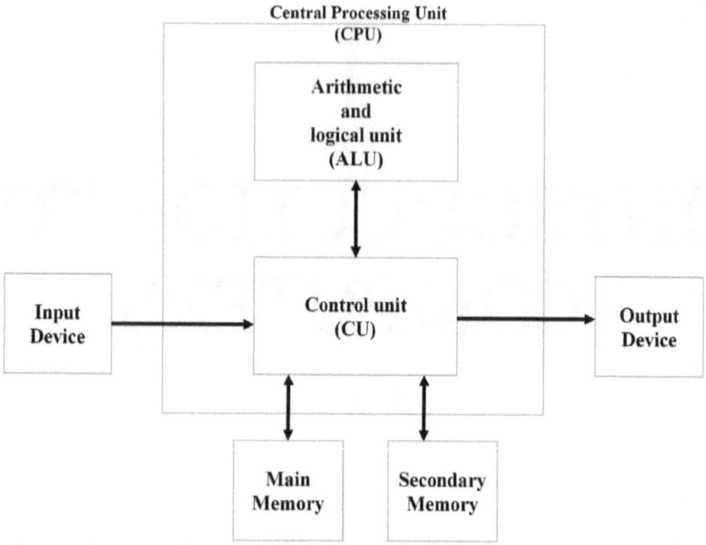

Figure 1.1 Central processing Unit

1. *Input Device:*

- Computer takes the data and instructions through an input device.
- And Convert that data and instructions into computer understandable.
- Input device gives that converted data and instructions for further processing.

Example: Keyboard, Mouse, Touch Screen, Scanner, Joy Stick, Webcam.

2. *Central Processing Unit(CPU) :*

- CPU is the brain of the computer and the most expensive part.
- Currently, CPUs are constructed as a single microchip, Where is referred to as a microprocessor.
- The CPU consists of two essential subunits.

(A) Control Unit(CU)
(B) Arthematic and logical unit(ALU)

(A) Control Unit(CU):
It is the central Nervous System.

- It controls, directs, and monitors the overall operations of the computer.
- The control unit instructs the input unit, on where to store the data after receiving it from the user unit.
- CU controls the flow of data and instructions from the storage unit to ALU.
- It also controls the flow of results from ALU to the storage unit.
- It tells other parts of a computer what to do.

(B) Arthematic and Logical Unit(ALU):

- The ALU Performs all the computations such as addition, Subtraction, Comparision, and so on. (+,-,*,/,>,<=)
- It performs all logical operations.
- It controls the speed of calculations.

3. *Storage Unit:*

- The storage unit of a computer holds data and instructions that are entered through the input unit before they are processed.
- It stores programs, data as well as intermediate results and results for output.
- its main function is to store information.

->The storage device can be divided into two main categories:
(A) Primary storage.
(B)Secondary storage.

(A) Primary Storage:
* It is also called main memory (or) Internal memory.
* It is Expensive, Smaller in size and faster.

* It has limited storage capacity.

* It is generally used to store the program being currently executed on the computer.

* It can store the data received from the input device.

* It can store intermediate and final results of the program.

* The primary memory is temporary.

* The data is lost when the computer is switched off.

* The CPU can access it directly at a very fast speed.

* The Primary Storage has limited storage capacity because it is very expensive and generally made up of semiconductor devices.

Example: RAM, ROM.

RAM:

- Random-access memory.
- It is volatile.
- The data in RAM are lost when the device is switched off.
- Data can be read and written.

ROM:

- Read-only memory.
- It is non-volatile.
- The data are not lost when the device switches off.
- Data can be read-only, but we can write.

(B) Secondary Storage:

*It is also known as external memory (or) Auxiliary memory.

* It stores operating system, data files, compiler, assembles, application programs etc.

* If CPU needs data present in secondary memory to main memory.

* It is a mass storage memory, slower but cheaper.

* It is non-volatile,

Example: Hard disk, pen drive, CD, DVD.

4. Output Unit:

* It mainly performs two operations.

1. It provides/gives information and results of computation to the outside world through the output unit.

2. It is used to convert the information and result into human-understandable.

Example: Monitors, Printers, Speakers, Projectors.

2. CREATING AND RUNNING PROGRAMS

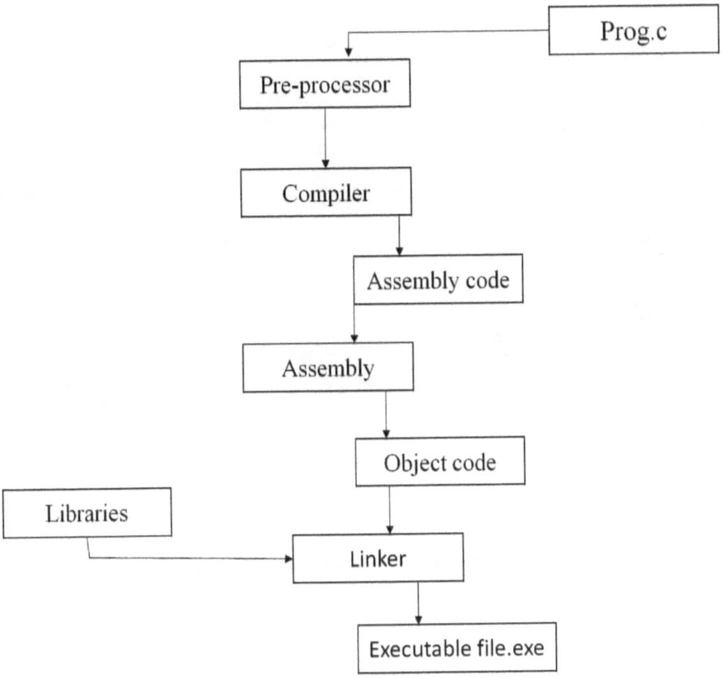

Figure 1.2 Flow of Creating and Running programs

Preprocessor :

In this phase, the source code is passed through the preprocessor. This phase includes :

- Preprocessor Remove comments
- Replace Macro Name with code
- Expansion of included Files(#include< >)

*The Preprocessor will convert high-level language to pur high-level language.

The Actual code before preprocess : (prog.c)

```
/*
*This is a sample addition program
*/
#include<stdio.h>
void main()
{
int a=10,b=5,c;
c=a+b;
printf("%d",c);
}
```

To see the result of the preprocessor stage,pass-E option gcc-E prog.c.
In the above example, the preprocessor will produce the context of the stdio.h header file joined with contexts of the prog.c.
After running the preprocessor the code looks like this.

Code of stdio.h

```
void main()
{
int a=10,b=5,c;
c=a+b;
printf("%d",c)
}
```

Compiler:

• It is 2nd stage of the compilation.

• In this stage the preprocessor code(pure high level) is translated to assembly code.

• This is intermediate human-readable language.

To solve the result of the compilation stage, pass-S option to gcc:

gcc - S prog.c

This will create a file named prog.s .This prog.s contains the generated assembly code.

Before Compiler

```
Code of stdio.h file
void main()
{
int a=10,b=5,c;
c=a+b;
printf("%d",c);
}
```

This is pure high-level code.

After the compiler runs(Assemble code)

```
Mov a,10
Mov b,5
ADD a,b
Call printf
leave
```

This is assembler code.

Assembler:

- This is 3rd stage of compilation.

- During the Assembly stage, an assembler is used to convert the assembly code into Machine code or object.

To see the result of the assembly stage, pass the –c option to gcc.
gcc-c prog.c
Running the above command will create a file named prog.o.The prog.o contains the object code of this program.

Before Assembler runs:

Mov a,10
Mov b,5
ADD a,b
Calls printf
leave

This is the Assembly code.

After Assembler Runs:

10---->1 0 1 0
5---->0 1 0 1
15----> 1 1 1 1
This is object code or machine code.

Linker:

- This is the final stage of compilation.
- It takes one or more object files or libraries as input and combines them to produce a single file.

3.COMPUTER NUMBERING SYSTEM

- Here we have 5 rules in the number system.

Rule 1 :

*"In this rule1, if we want to convert binary to decimal, octal to decimal and hexadecimal to decimal then we should use the method of the **weighted sum of each digit position.**"*

Examples:

Binary to Decimal :

1. $(1001)_2 = (\ ?\ )_{10}$

We should convert binary to decimal by using the weighted sum of each digit position i.e,

Binary digit * (2 to the power of digit position)

Note : From L.S.B(Least Significant Bit) is $2^0, 2^1, 2^2, 2^3 \ldots\ldots 2^n$.

Now,

$(1001)_2 = 1 \times 2^3 + 0 \times 2^2 + 0 \times 2^1 + 1 \times 2^0$

$= 8 + 0 + 0 + 1$

$= 9$

$\therefore (1001)_2 = (\ 9\ )_{10}$

2. $(101.011)_2 = (\ ?\ )10$

Break down the above binary number **$(101.011)_2$** into 2 parts.

Here, 101 is the Integral part and 011 is the fractional part.

- From left to the binary point give digit positions like $2^0, 2^1, 2^2, 2^3 \ldots\ldots 2^n$.

  Then the result is, $1 \times 2^2 + 0 \times 2^1 + 1 \times 2^0 = 5$

- From right to the binary point give digit position like

  $2^{-1}, 2^{-2}, 2^{-3}, 2^{-4} \ldots\ldots 2^{-n}$.

  Then the result is, $0 \times 2^{-1} + 1 \times 2^{-2} + 1 \times 2^{-3} = 0.375$

  $\therefore (101.011)_2 = (\ 5.375\ )10$

Octal to Decimal :

1. $(3208)_8 = (?)_{10}$

Here, **Binary digit * (8 to the power of digit position)**

Note : From L.S.B(Least Significant Bit) is $8^0, 8^1, 8^2, 8^3 .....8^n$

$(3208)_8 = 3 \times 8^3 + 2 \times 8^2 + 0 \times 8^1 + 8 \times 8^0 = 208$

∴ **$(3208)_8 = (208)_{10}$**

2. $(357.72)_8 = (?)_{10}$

Break down the above binary number **$(357.72)_8$** into 2 parts.

Here, 357 is the Integral part and 72 is the fractional part.

- From left to the decimal point give digit positions like $8^0, 8^1, 8^2, 8^3 .....8^n$

Then the result is, $3 \times 8^2 + 5 \times 8^1 + 7 \times 8^0 = 239$

- From right to the decimal point give digit position like

$8^{-1}, 8^{-2}, 8^{-3}, 8^{-4} .....8^{-n}$.

Then the result is, $7 \times 8^{-1} + 2 \times 8^{-2} = 0.906$

∴ $(357.72)_8 = (239.906)_{10}$

Hexadecimal to Decimal :

Here, **Binary digit * (16 to the power of digit position)**

Note: From L.S.B(Least Significant Bit) is $16^0, 16^1, 16^2, 16^3 .....16^n$.

1. $(565)_{16} = (?)_{10}$

$(565)_{16} = 5 \times 16^2 + 6 \times 16^1 + 5 \times 16^0 = 1381$

∴ $(565)_{16} = (1381)_{10}$

2. $(16.3B)_{16} = (?)_{10}$

Break down the above binary number **$(16.B)_{16}$** into 2 parts.

Here, 16 is the Integral part and 3B is the fractional part.

- From left to the decimal point give digit positions like $16^0, 16^1, 16^2, 16^3 .....16^n$

Then the result is, $1 \times 16^1 + 6 \times 16^0 = 22$

- From right to the decimal point give digit position like

  $16^{-1}, 16^{-2}, 16^{-3}, 16^{-4}.....16^{-n}$.
  Here, B is 11.
  Then the result is, $3 \times 16^{-1} + 11 \times 16^{-2} = 0.230$
  $\therefore$ **$(16.3B)_{16} = (22.230)_{10}$**

Rule 2 :

> *"In Rule 2, if we want to convert decimal to any number system use the method of repeatedly dividing by 2 for binary (or) 8 for octal (or) 16 for hexadecimal and then collect the remainders"*

Examples :

Decimal to Binary :

1. $(305)_{10} = (\ )_2$

1. Divide the given number by 2 then it gives the resulting quotient along with the remainder i.e,(the very first remainder is LSB)

2. Repeatedly divide the result (Quotient) until result (Quotient) will be zero

302 / 2 = 152 (Remainder is 1)
152 / 2 = 76 (Remainder is 0)
76 / 2 = 38 (Remainder is 0)
38 / 2 = 19 (Remainder is 0)
19 / 2 = 9 (Remainder is 1)
9 / 2 = 4 (Remainder is 1)
4 / 2 = 2 (Remainder is 0)
2 / 2 = 1 (Remainder is 0)
1 / 2 = 0 (Remainder is 1)

3. Collect the remainder from the bottom (LSB) to the top (MSB)
$(100110001)_2$

2. $(250.58)_{10} = (\ )_2$

- Firstly divide integral part 250 out of (250.58) by 2

250 / 2 = 125 (Remainder is 0)
125 / 2 = 62 (Remainder is 1)
62 / 2 = 31 (Remainder is 0)
31 / 2 = 15 (Remainder is 1)
15 / 2 = 7 (Remainder is 1)
7 / 2 = 3 (Remainder is 1)3 / 2 = 1 (Remainder is 1)
1 / 2 = 0(Remainder is 1)

- Secondly multiply fractional part 0.58 out of (250.58) by 2 until the number becomes zero
- Collect the integral part values from top to bottom

0.59 X 2 = 1.16
0.16 X 2 = 0.32
0.32 X 2 = 0.64
0.64 X 2 = 1.28
0.28 X 2 = 0.56
= (250.58) =(1111010.10010)

Decimal to Octal :

1. $(266)_{10} = ( )_8$

1. Divide the given number 266 by 8 then it gives the result (quotient) along with the remainder i.e,(the very first remainder is LSB)

2. Repeatedly divide the result (quotient) until the result (quotient) will be zero

3. Collect the remainders from bottom (LSB) to top (MSB)
266 / 8 =33 (Remainder is 2)
33 / 8 = 4 (Remainder is 1)
4 / 8 = 0 (Remainder is 4)

- $(412)_8$

2. $(266.612)_{10} = ( )_8$

* 266 conversion has already done in above .So we need to calculate only for Integral part

* After calculating the integral part collect the integral part from top to bottom

0.612 X 8 = 4.896

0.896 X 8 = 7.168

0.168 X 8 = 1.344

0.344 X 8 = 2.752

0.752 X 8 = 6.016

0.016 X 8 = 0.128

$(266.612)_{10} = (412.471260)_8$

3.Decimal to Hexa Decimal :

(i). $(912)_{10} = ( )_{16}$

912 / 16 = 57 (Remainder is 0)

57 / 16 = 3 (Remainder is 9)

3 / 16 = 0 (Remainder is 3)

- Now collect the remainders from LSB to MSB

$(390)_{16}$

Rule 3:

"In rule 3, if we want to convert binary to octal and binary to hexadecimal then divide the 3 bits for octal as a group and 4 bits for hexadecimal"

Examples:

Binary to Octal

1. $(01011.100)_8 = ( )_8$

*Initially start the grouping of 3 bits from the left side to the right side of a integral part.

*Secondly start the grouping of three bits from the right side to the left side of the factorial part.

*Lastly convert the group of 3-bit binary digits to its relevant octal digit

$(01\ 011.100)_2$

$=> (13.4)_8$

Binary to Hexadecimal

*Initially start the grouping of 4 bits from the right side to the left side of an integral part

*Secondly start the grouping of 4 bits from the left side to the right side of a fractional part

*Lastly convert the group of 4 bits binary digits to its relevant hexadecimal

(0010 0000 1100.1010 1110)

$(20C.AE)_{16}$

Rule 4:

> *"In rule 4, if we want to convert octal to binary then convert each octal digit then convert each octal digit to its relevant 3-bit binary number and hexadecimal to binary then convert each hexadecimal to 4-bit binary number"*

Examples:

Octal to Binary :

1. $(231.317)_8 = ( )_2$?

Integral Part Conversion

2's Binary number is 010

3's Binary number is 011

1's Binary number is 001

Fractional Part Conversion

3' s Binary number is 011

1's Binary number is 001

7's Binary number is 111

*Initially start converting each digit of the integral part to its relevant 3-bit binary number

*Secondly start converting each digit of the fractional part to its relevant 3-bit binary number

$(231.317)_8 = (010\ 011\ 001.011\ 001\ 111)_2$

Hexadecimal to Binary:

1. $(DE.9F)_{16} = (\ )_2$

*Here D = 13, E = 14, F = 15

*Initially start converting each digit of the integral part to its relevant 4-bit binary number

*Secondly start converting each digit of the fractional part to its relevant 4-bit binary number

$(0001\ 0011\ 0001\ 0100.1001\ 0001\ 0101)_2$

Rule 5:

"In rule 5, if we want to convert octal to hexadecimal and hexadecimal to octal, firstly convert that number to binary and then convert that binary to its desired number system."

Examples:

Octal to Hexadecimal:

1. $(4071)_8 = (\ )_{16}$?

*Initially start converting each digit to a 3-bit binary number

$(100\ 000\ 111\ 001)_2$

*Secondly start grouping off 4 bits from right side to left side

$(1000\ 0011\ 1001)_2$

*Lastly convert the group of 4 bits binary to its relevant hexadecimal Number

$(839)_{16}$

2. $(124.76)_8 = (\ )_{16}$

- Initially start converting each digit of the integral part as well as fractional part to its relevant 3-bit binary number

$(001\ 010\ 100\ .111\ 110)_2$

- Secondly start grouping of 4 bits from the right side (LSB) to the left side (MSB) of an integral part and vice-versa for the fractional part

$(001\ 010\ 100.111\ 110)_2$

Note: In case we get a shortage of digits while grouping into 4 bits remaining as zeros

$(0000\ 0101\ 0100.1111\ 1000)_2$

- Convert above each 4-bit binary group into its desired number system

$(054.F8)_{16}$

Hexadecimal to Octal:

1. $(C1F.F8)_{16} = (\ )_8$

- Initially start converting each digit of the integral part as well as fractional part to its relevant 4-bit binary number

$(1100\ 0001\ 1111.1111\ 1000)_2$

- Secondly start grouping of 3 bits from the right side (LSB) to the left side(MSB) of an integral part and vice-versa for the fractional part

$(110\ 000\ 011\ 111.111\ 110\ 000)_2$

- Convert above each 3-bit binary group into its desired number system

$(6037.760)_8$

4. STORING INTEGERS :

"Storing integers means, how we can store the integer values in computer memory."

Here we have 2 types of integers:-

i. Unsigned integers
ii. Signed integers

Unsigned Integers :

We can store the unsigned integers in an easy or straightforward process.

- Firstly convert the given number into its corresponding binary numbers

  Example :
  Let us take 4-bit integers which can store 0 to 15 numbers.
  Example: storing number 4 in computer
  Addition of two unsigned integers :
  Take A=4, and B=6 to add two numbers (A+B) is just an easy process.
  A = 4 = 0 1 0 0
  B = 6 = 0 1 1 0
  A+B=10=1010

Signed Integer Storing :

Storing signed integers is very much different from storing unsigned integers. Signed integers have positive and negative numbers

- An unsigned integer is a straightforward process, but a signed integer is a difficult process.

  Here we have 3 methods for storing signed integer numbers:-

- Sign and magnitude

- 1's complement
- 2's complement

1. Sign and Magnitude :

The most significant bit(MSB) is used as a sign bit.
If MSB is zero, this means it is a positive number.
If MSB is one, this means it is a negative number.

The syntax for sign-magnitude form :

Sign Bit	Actual Binary

If we want to represent +6 value in 4-bit :

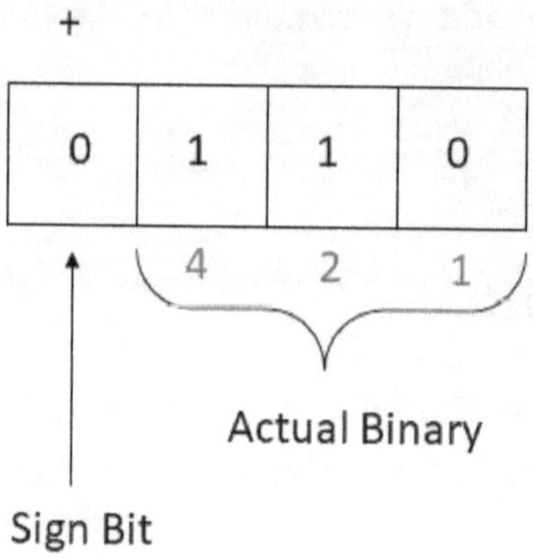

If we want to represent +6 value in 4-bit :

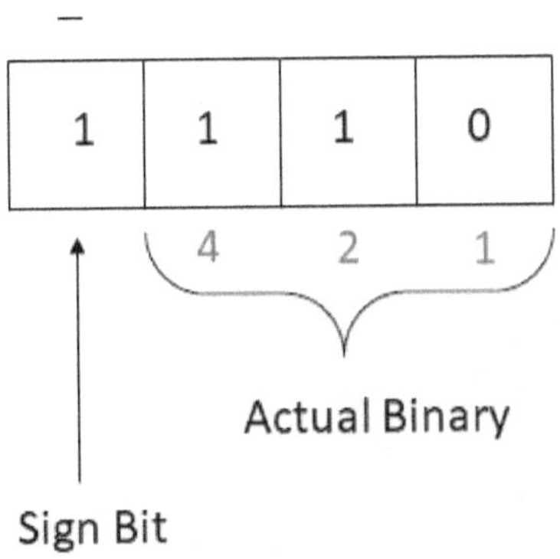

Example 1 :
Take A = +4 and B = +2, now **A + B** is :

$$A = +4 = 0\ 1\ \ 0\ 0$$
$$B = +2 = 0\ 0\ \ 1\ 0$$

$$+6 = 0\ 1\ 1\ 0$$

Example 2 :
Take A = - 4 and B = +2, now **- A + B** is :

$$
\begin{array}{r}
A = -4 = 1\ 1\ 0\ 0 \\
B = +2 = 0\ 0\ 1\ 0 \\
\hline
-2 = 1\ 1\ 1\ 0 \\
\hline
\end{array}
$$

2. 1's Complement :

A1's complement and 2's complement are used to store signed integer numbers in computer memory.

Role of 1's complement in storing numbers :

1's complement is used to represent a signed binary number.

It is used to perform arithmetic operations like addition and subtraction.

Consider a 4-bit integer.

Number	Binary rep	Number	1's Compliment
+0	0000	-0	1111
+1	0001	-1	1110
+2	0010	-2	1101
+3	0011	-3	1100
+4	0100	-4	1011
+5	0101	-5	1010
+6	0110	-6	1001
+7	0111	-7	1000

Table 1.1 1's complement

Properties :

1. The MSB represents 0 for positive and 1 for negative.
2. This method contains two zeroes, one is +0(0000) another one is -0(1111).

Addition :

A = +3 = 0 0 1 1

B = -2 = 1 1 0 1

A+B= 5 = 0 1 0 1

To add (A + B) we just add the numbers bit by bit.

Subtraction :

To subtract (A - B) we just add A and the 1's complement of B.

Here, A - B is equals to A + (- B).

A = +3 = 0 0 1 1

B = -2 = 1 1 0 1 → 1's compliment of 2

A + (-B) = 1 1 0 0 0 0

→ 1

0 0 0 1

Here we must add the carry produced in the last column to the result.

If there is no carry, add minus to the 1's complement of the sum obtained.

Role of 2's complement in storing numbers :

This is another method to represent negative binary numbers.

i. The MSB(most significant bit) represents "0" for positive and "1" for negative.
ii. 2's complement has only one zero (0000).
iii. Here we have 2 operations to change the sign of a number.

a. Firstly convert the given number into 1's complement
b. Lastly, add 1 to the 1's complement

i. Here addition and subtraction are very easy.
ii. To add two numbers (A+B) just simply add the numbers bit by bit.
iii. To subtract two numbers (A-B), then add 2's complement of B to A.

Addition :-

A = 3 = 0 0 1 1
B = 2 = 0 0 1 0
+5 = 0 1 0 1

Subtraction :-

Find subtraction of 0011(3) and 0010(2) using 2's complement
Here,
A = 0 0 1 1
B = 0 0 1 0
Need to find A-B, i.e, A+(-B) i.e, A+ (2's complement of B).

i. Firstly calculate the 2's complement of B i.e, 0010
ii. 1's complement of B 0010 is 1101
iii. Add +1 to the 1's complement (1101)

1 1 0 1
+1
1 1 1 0
Note :- 2's complement is nothing but adding 1 to the 1's complement
Now add 2's complement of B to A
A = 0 0 1 1
2's complement of B = 1 1 1 0
Carry bit 1 0 0 0 1
In 2's complement, the leftmost bit of the result is called carry and it is ignored.
So, the answer is :- 0 0 0 1

5. STORING REAL NUMBERS :

"Real numbers are stored in computer memory by using Sign(S), Exponent (E), and Mantissa (M)."

1. Sign
2. Exponent
3. Mantissa

1. Sign :

MSB is used as a sign bit.
If MSB is 0, this means it is a positive number
If MSB is 1 this means it is a negative number

2.Exponent :

The exponent (power of 2)defines the power.
The power should be positive or negative

3. Mantissa :

The Mantissa is the binary number.
The Mantissa Present right of the binary point.
Precision is a floating-point number that depends on the number of bits used to represent mantissa.
The mantissa is stored as an unsigned integer
We can say that the original number N is
$N = (-1)^s * 1.M * 2^e$
Where s is a sign, M is mantissa and e is the exponent

IEEE standards for floating-point representation :

Here we have 2 standards to store a floating-point number in Computer memory.

1. Single precision
2. Double precision

1. Single-Precision

In a 32 bit single Precision we have 1 bit for sign bit (0 Or 1), exponent which has 8 bits, and 23 bits for mantissa part

Sign 1 Bit	Exponent (8 bits + excess 27)	Mantissa (23 bits)

2. *Double precision*

In a 64-bit double Precision, we have one bit for signing it (0 or 1),11 bits for the exponent, and 52bits for the mantissa.

Sign 1 Bit	Exponent (11 bits + excess 1023)	Mantissa (52 bits)

For example to store 263.3 in computer memory using IEEE single precision

1. Given real number is 263.3
2. Find the binary value for the integral part that is 263.

263 /2 = 131 (Remainder is 1)
131 /2 = 65 (Remainder is 1)
65 / 2 = 32(Remainder is 1)
32 /2 = 16 (Remainder is 0)
16 / 2 = 8 (Remainder is 0)
8 / 2 = 4 (Remainder is 0)
4 / 2 = 2(Remainder is 0)
2 / 2 = 1 (Remainder is 0)
1 / 2 = 0 (Remainder is 1)
$(263.3)_{10}$ = $(1 0 0 0 0 0 1 1 1)_2$

3. Find the binary value for the fractional part that is 0.3

We can find binary value by multiplying fractional part 0.3 by 2 until the number becomes zero.

And also collect the integral part values from top to bottom

Multiply by 2	Integral part	Decimal point	Fractional Part
0.3 x 2	0	.	6
0.6 x 2	1	.	2
0.2 x 2	0	.	4
0.4 x 2	0	.	8
0.8 x 2	1	.	6
0.6 x 2	1	.	2

Table 1.2 binary value for the fractional part

$(263.3)_{10} \Rightarrow (100000111.010011..)_2$

4. Move the binary point towards the left up to MSB and count how many places did the binary point moves in this case the binary point moves 8 places towards the left up to MSB

$N = 1.00000111010011... \times 2^8$

1	10000111	00000111010011
Sign Bit	8 bit Exponent	23 bit mantissa

Excess 127 + 8 bit

$= (135)_{10}$

In the above representation

- The sign bit is 1.
- Exponent comes is 10000111 it is obtained by adding excess 127 + size of the exponent is 8 bit that equals to 135 and converts 135 to a binary field that 135 binary number(100001111) in place of the exponent.
- Mantissa means 23-bit binary number i.e, binary number present right to binary point.

6. INTRODUCTION TO C :

The C language is a high-level programming language developed by **Dennis Ritchie** in 1972 at Bell Laboratories.

The UNIX operating system was developed in C language i.e., (95% in C &5% in assembly language). C is called general-purpose programming language, i.e., general-purpose means, this can be used for many purposes like mathematical calculations, research work, application development, UNIX operating system design, etc. It is very easy to understand when compared to Machine language and Assembly language.

C Language is a collection of functions where one function is mandatory which is the main() function. That's why C is called modular programming language, i. e. dividing a large program into small chunks is called modular programming.

Features of C Language

1. **Simple:** C is a simple programming language because it is easy to understand and, modify when compared to machine and assembly language and here large programs are divided into smaller parts to understand the code easily.

2. **Portable:** This is nothing but machine-independent. Here there is a provision that the code written on one machine can run or execute on another machine. For example in system A user/programmer writes the sum of two numbers program and takes that code from system A and executes it in system B, then it executes/runs successfully without any errors due to portability.

3. **Middle-Level Programming Language:** Yes, the C language is a middle-level language because it can support both high level and assembler programming languages, that's why we can call itas a middle-level programming language.

Example:

```
#include<stdio. h>
    void main()
```

```
{
int p=2, d=4, output;
_asm_
{
mov ax, p
mov bx, d
add ax, bx
mov output, ax
}
printf("value after addition is:%d", output);
}
```

In the above program, we write inline assemble language in C.

1. In main () function declares variables p, d, and output, and p holds 2 and d holds 4.
2. After that write assemble language in the main () function using the _asm_ keyboard.
3. Assemble language works on the register, here value in p is copied to register ax and similarly value in d is copied to register bx and adds the values of two registers i. e., ax and bx.
4. After that, the value in the ax register is copied into variable output,
5. Finally, print the value in the variable output using the printf () function.

7. TRANSLATORS

Every high-level language needs a translator to convert a high-level language to machine understandable language."The translator is a software to convert a high-level language to lower-level language/machine understandable language."

Here we have mainly 3 translators

- Compiler
- Assembler
- Interpreter

Compiler

- A compiler is a software that converts high-level language source programs to machine-understandable language/object code.
- The compiler takes a total source program as a single input and gives all the errors of the source program at a time.

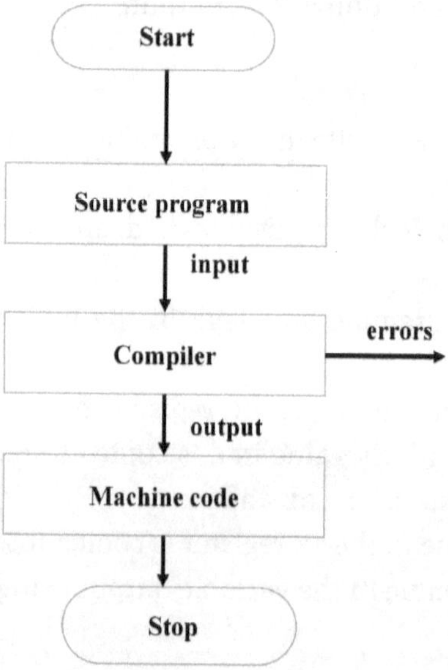

Figure 1.3 Flow chart of Compiler

Assembler

- An assembler is a software, that converts assemble language source programs to machine understandable code/ object code.
- The assembler takes a total source program as a single input and gives all the errors of a source program at a time.

Example: Assemble language

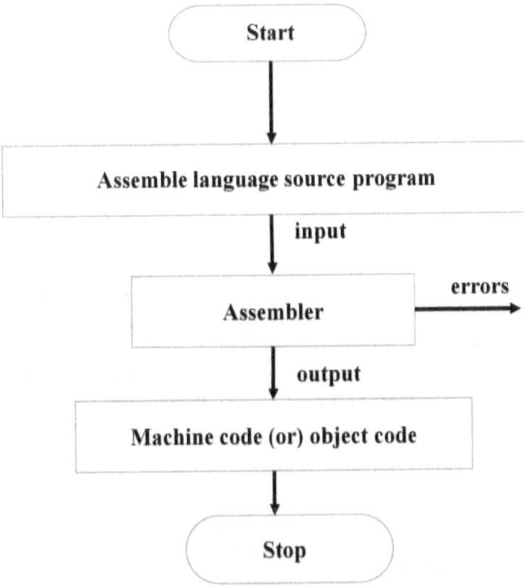

Figure 1.4 Flowchart of Assembler

Interpreter

- Interpreter is software that converts high-level language source programs to machine-understandable language/object code line by line.
- An interpreter takes a single line of a program as an input and if no error is found in that line the interpreter converts it into object code and takes another line of a program to translate up to the end of the program or any error found. In case any error occurs at a particular line then the interpreter stops converting and shows that error.

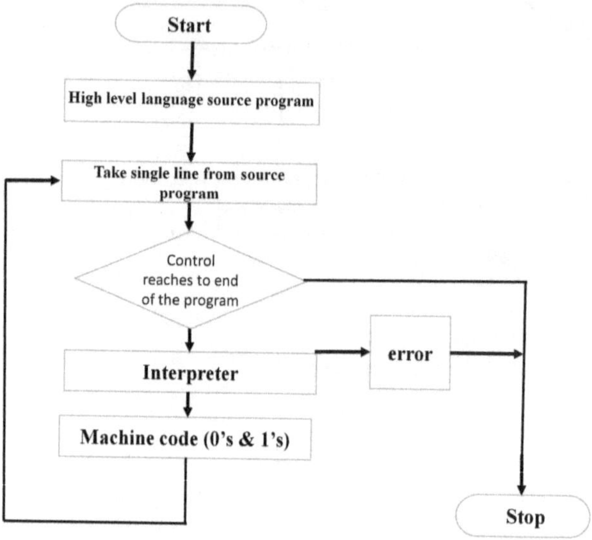

Figure 1.5 Flowchart of Interpreter

8. IDENTIFIERS

The identifier is nothing but names of a variable, functions, arrays, structures, etc. The identifier cannot be a keyword in C.

For Example

```
int patient_id;
void area_circle()
{
// statements;
}
struct patient_details
{
//structure members
}
int array[20];
```

In the above examples

patient_id, area_circle, patient_details, and array are the identifiers.

Rules for Identifiers

1. The identifier name must not start with a digit.
2. Identifier names can contain digits anywhere in the name but do not start with a digit.
3. The identifier name should be a collection of ***alphabets*** (A-Z, a-z) and we may use special characters like ***underscore*** (_) between alphabets instead of ***blank space.***
4. The identifier name does not agree with **Blank Space.**
5. The identifier name must not agree on any keywords.

9. DATA TYPES

> "*"A data type states the type of data that can be stored (holds) by the Variable."*"

Basic Data Types:-

1. int
2. char
3. float
4. double

Derived Data Types:-

1. Array
2. Pointers
3. Structure
4. Union

Enumeration Data Types:-

1. Enum.

Void Data Type:-

1. Void

Let's see the sizes and ranges of a basic data type in the following table.

A C program to print size and range of different data types.

```
/*A c program to find size and range of a data type */
#include <stdio.h>
#include <limits.h>
#include <float.h>
int main()
{
printf("char\t %d byte\t %d to %d\n", sizeof(char), CHAR_MIN,
CHAR_MAX);
printf("int\t %d byte\t %d to %d\n", sizeof(int), INT_MIN, INT_MAX);
printf("float\t %d byte\t %d to %d\n", sizeof(float), FLT_MIN, FLT_MAX);
printf("double\t %d byte\t %d to %d\n", sizeof(double), DBL_MIN,
DBL_MAX);
return 0;
}
```

Output:-

```
char 1 byte -128 to 127
int 4 byte -2147483648 to 2147483647
float 4 byte 1.17549e-38 to 3.40282e+38
double 8 byte 2.22507e-308 to 1.79769e+308
```

Explanation:-

In the above program, at pre processor directive.

We have two libraries i.e. #include<limits.h> and#include<float.h>.

Firstly, the variables CHAR_MIN, CHAR_MAX, INT_MIN AND INT_MAX is present in standard library #include <limits.h>. Here CHAR_MIN and INT_MIN says that the minimum value stored in char and int variables respectively.

Secondly, the variables FLT_MIN, FLT_MAX, DBL_MIN and DBL_MAX is present in preprocessor directive #include <float.h>. Here FLT_MIN, and

DBL_MIN say that the minimum value is stored in float and double type variables respectively, and FLT_MAX, and DBL_MAX say that the maximum value is stored in float and double type variables respectively.

Finally, by using the above variables we can see the minimum values a variable can store.

10. VARIABLES

> *"Variables means name given to a memory location that holds data based on type. Variables can be able to wrap up data in the main memory or shortage area."*

In this memory location has a name (should follow rules to give a name) and address, which holds data.

Rules For Variable Name :

Digit:

1. The variable name must not start with a digit.

   For example, **int 9std_roll**; is an invalid declaration because it starts with a digit.

2. Variable names can contain digits anywhere in the name but do not start with a digit. For example, **int std_roll9;** is a valid declaration, because the variable name doesn't start with a digit.

Alphabets and Underscore:

The variable name should be a collection of ***alphabets*** (A-Z, a-z) and we may use special characters like ***underscore*** **(_)** between alphabets instead of ***blank space.***

For example, **int std_roll**; Or **int stroll**; is a valid declaration.

No Blank Space:

The variable name does not agree with the **blank space.**

For example, **int std name;** is invalid, because there is a blank space between "std" and "name".

No Keywords:

The variable name must not agree to any keywords.

For example, **int extern;** is invalid because "extern" is a keyword.

Case Sensitive:

C program is a case-sensitive language, uppercase characters are dissimilar to lower case characters.

For example, intstd_roll, int STD_ROLL, and int std_ROLL, these three variables are different from each other. For these *three* variables contains *three* different memories will be allocated.

Syntax to Declare Variable

datatype variable_name;

For example

int roll;

Here "rollno" is a variable name of type integer.

float marks;

Here "marks" is a variable name of type floating decimal.

char gender;

Here "gender" is a variable name of type character.

Syntax to Variable Initialization

datatype variable_name = value;

For example

1. int rollno = 1248; It is integer variable initialization.
2. float marks = 78.25; It is float variable initialization.
3. char gender='M'; It is character variable initialization.

In a **C** program, mainly we have 2 types of variables,

1. Local Variable
2. Global Variable

Local Variable :

> *"A variable that is present within the function is known as a local variable. It is impossible to access the local variable from the out of the function because the scope of the local variable is within the function only."*

- The default value of a local variable is garbage.
- For local variables, memory will be allocated in the stack area.
- The lifetime of the local variable is in between function start and function end.
- Local variable data can be stored at the stack area in RAM (main memory).

Example program for local variable:-

```
#include <stdio.h>
int main()
{
//local variable declaration
int roll_no;
float marks;
char gender;
// variable initialization.
roll_no=1248;
marks=89.26;
gender='M';
printf("Roll_no:%d\n Marks:%f\n Gender:%c\n", roll_no, marks, gender);
return 0;
}
```

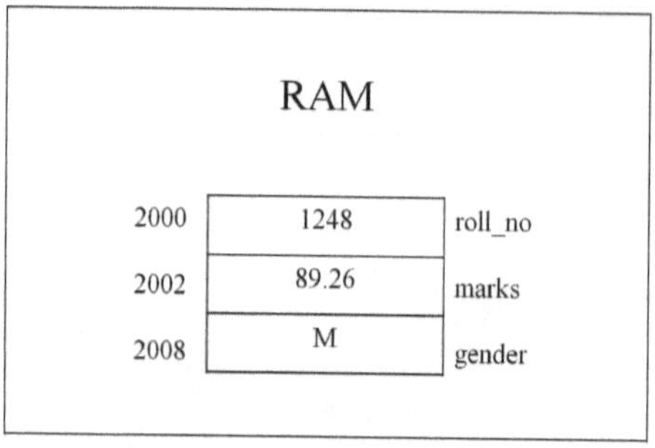

Figure 1.6 Memory allocation

Output:-

Roll_no:1248
Marks:89.260002
Gender: M

Explanation:-

In the above program, there are 3 local variables are declared and initialized. Whenever the control evaluates the statement **int roll_no;** the compiler allocates 2 or 4 bytes of memory on stack and memory allocation depends on system configuration(memory allocation diagram shown above) the scope of **roll_no** variable is with in the main() function.

- Next compiler excutes **float marks;** the compiler allocates 4 bytes of memory and scope is within the function.
- Again compiler excutes **char gender;** the compiler allocates 1 byte of memory.
- Again compiler excutes, variable initialization steps and initialized values are stored in memory.
- Above 3 variables are local to the **main() function,** the lifetime of local Variable startsfrom open bracket({) and ends with closed brackets (}).

Global Variable:-

"A variable which is present outside the function or above the main () function is called a global variable."

- The scope of global variable is throughout the program.
- The default value of global variable is zero.

- Global variable data can be stored in variable section at RAM (main memory).

Example program for global variable:-

```
#include <stdio.h>
int roll_no; //global variable of type integer.
float marks; //global variable of type floating.
char gender; //global variable of type character.
int main()
{
//variable initialization
roll_no=1248;
marks=89.26;
gender='M';
printf("Roll no:%d\n Marks:%f\n Gender:%c", roll_no, marks, gender);
return 0;
}
```

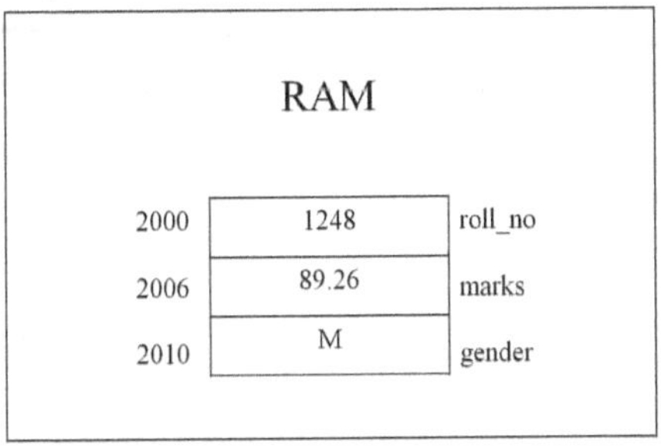

Figure 1.7 Memory allocation

Output:

Roll no:1248
Marks:89.260002
Gender:M

Explanation:

Here ***int roll_no, float marks*** and ***char gender*** are global variables of type integer, floating decimal and character respectively, and default value of these variables is zero. Next control will enter into *main ()* function, and evaluates int roll_no=1248, float marks=89.26 and char gender='M' respectively, after that these values are stored in a global area section in RAM.

Next control evaluates ***printf("Roll no:%d\n marks:%f\n gender:%c", roll_no, marks, gender);***

This statement prints data present in global variables.

Case Study on Variables

Case1: Global variable and local variable names are different

```
#include <stdio.h>
int a=10;
void main()
{
int b=40;
printf("Global variable:%d\n", a);
printf("Local variable:%d\n", b);
}
```

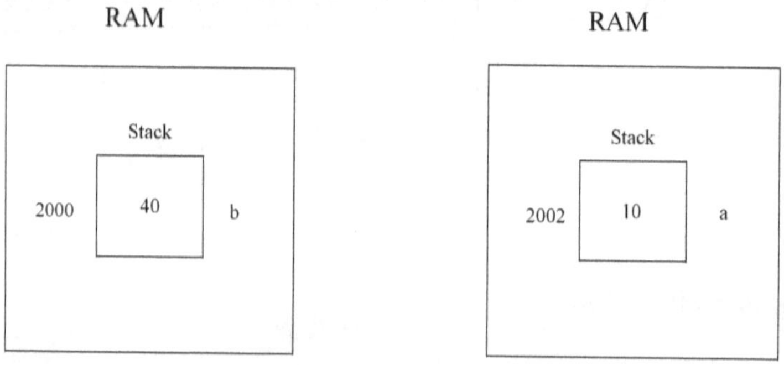

Figure 1.8 Memory allocation

Output:-

Global variable:10

Local variable:40

Explanation:

In the above case local and global variable names are different.

- Initially the compiler evaluate **int a=10**; (Global variable) section of RAM.
- After evaluate **int b=40**;(Local variable) the memory will allocates in the stack area of RAM.
- After evaluating **print** statements, the global and local variable data fetch from a global variable section and stock area section respectively.

Case2:- Global variable and local variable names are same:-

```
#include <stdio.h>
int a=10; //global variable
void main()
{
int a=40; //local variable
printf("a=%d", a);
}
```

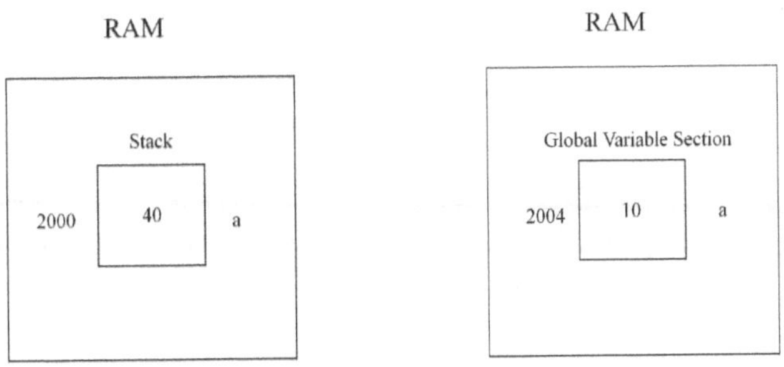

Figure 1.9 Memory allocation

Output :

a=40

In the above case local and global variable names are same. After evaluating **int a=10** (Global variable) statement the memory will allocate in global area section at RAM. After evaluating **int a=40** (Local variable) statement in main() function, the memory will allocate in the stack area of RAM.

After evaluating **printf("a=%d", a)**; statement, then compiler get an ambiguity that which "a" value it needs to print. As of rule compiler gives 1st preference to local variable instead of global variable due to that output is 40.

Note:-

Memory locations of Local variable and Global variable are different, due to this compiler does not show an error.

Case3:-What happens if local variable names are same.

```
#include <stdio.h>
   int main()
   {
   int a=10; //local variable
   int a=40;
   printf("a=%d\n", a);
   }
```

Output:-

error: redefinition of 'a'
int a=40;

Explanation

In the above program, If a compiler found the same variables names in a single block or a function then ambiguity will occur and issues an error saying that "**error: redefinition of 'a' int a=40** ".

11. CONSTANTS :

* Here we have five types of constants.

1. Integer constant.
2. Floating-point constant.
3. Octal and Hexadecimal constant.
4. Character constants.
5. String constant.

1. Integer Constants:

* It should be of any number.
    * It must not be a real number.
    * It can be of either negative or positive numbers.
    * It allows the range up to -32768 to 32767.
    [ex: const int a = 3.14]

Example:

```
main()
{
const int x =24;
print f ("%d",x);
}
```

2. Floating-point Constant:

* It can have a decimal point i.e; a value with an integer part and fractional part.
    * It can be either a positive or negative number.
    * It must not contain any commas and blank spaces in real constant.
    [const float b = 24.29;]

Example:

```
main()
{
const int x =24.29;
print f ("%f",x);
}
```

3. Character Constants:

- A single alphabet, any Single special character (@,/&...etc) and any digit enclosed in the single quotation is called character constant.
- The size of the character Constant is 1 bite. It Stores one character.

[ex: const char x='d';]

Example:

```
main()
{
const char x ='d';
print f ("%c",x);
}
```

4. String Constant:

- It is a collection of characters and enclosed in double-quotes.
- It may also contain special characters, digits, letters and escaped sequences in double-quotes.
- The string constant ends with a Null character '\0'.

[ex: const char a[10] = "ram";]

Example:

```
main()
{
const char x[10] ="manasa";
printf("%s",x);
}
```

5. Octal and Hexadecimal Constant:

* The base 8 number system is known as octal. The number range is from 0 to 7.

* Represent an octal constant value with zero.

ex:const int a = 024;

* The base 16 number system is known as hexadecimal. The number range is 0 to 9 and the letters A to F. A indicate 10,b is11,c is 12,d is 13,e is 14,f is 15.

*Represent an hexa constant value with 0 X [constant with hexadecimal form].

ex: const int a = 0 X 29;

const int a = 0 X 1AC;

Example:

```
main()
{
const int x =024;
const int y =0 X 1D;
print f ("octal =%d hexadecimal = %d",x,y);
}
```

12. INPUT / OUTPUT :

In C programming we have four standard library input and output functions are there

They are

1. printf( ) function
2. scanf( ) function
3. getchar( ) and putchar( ) function
4. gets( ) and puts( ) functions

printf( ) function :

1. This function is the most commonly used function in C language.
2. This function works under the STDIO.H header file.
3. The working of this function is to show the output on console.

Example:

```
#include <stdio.h>
void main( )
{
int a = 10,b = 20;
printf("Addition is %d ",a+b);
}
```

scanf( ) function :

1. This function is the most commonly used language.
2. This function works under the studio.h header file.
3. The working of this function is to take input from the console.

Example:

```
#include <stdio.h>
void main( )
{
int a;
printf("Enter a value ");
scanf("%d",&a);
}
```

getchar( ) and putchar( ) :

- getchar( ) and putchar( ) are non-standard functions.
- These functions works under stdio.h header file.
- The working of getchar( ) is gets a single character from stdin.
- The working of putchar( ) is to write a single character on console or screen.

Example :

```
#include <stdio.h>
void main( )
{
char ch;
printf("Enter a character");
ch = getchar( );
printf("Entered character is ");
puts(ch);
}
```

gets( ) and puts( ) functions :

- gets( ) and puts( ) functions are non-standard functions.

- These functions works under stdio.h header file.
- The working of gets( ) function is to read input and save it as a string .
- The working of puts( ) function is just same as printf( ) function and prints characters on a console (or) screen.

Example:

```
#include <stdio.h>
    void main( )
    {
    char a[100];
    //Read string from console
    printf("Enter a string");
    gets(a);
    //print string by using puts( )
    puts(a);
    }
```

13. SCOPE:

- *"Scope of a variable means up to where the variable can be accesable."*
- *"The total story of a scope evolve around whether the variuble is declared inside a function or outside a function."*

Scope of a variable means a particular portion or a place , where the variable can be accessed.

- In case, a variable is declared inside a function so that variable is local to that particular function.So,the scope of that particular variable is within that function only .

- In case,a variable is declared out a function so,that variable is global . So, the scope of that particular variable is throughout the program.

There are 3 types of Scopes:
1.Block Scope
2.Function Scope
3.File Scope

Block Scope:

- A variable which is declared inside a block and that particular variable has block scope.
- The variable inside a block cannot gives its access to outside.So,the scope of such a variable is within that block.
- This variable can access anywhere in the block.
- Where the block ends,there the scope ends.

Example:

```
#include<stdio.h>
void main()
{
//block
{
int a=10,b=20;
printf("%d",a);
}
printf("%d",b);
}
```

Explanation:

- Variable 'a' is assigned with 10 and 'b' is assigned with 20 in a block.

- The statement printf("%d",a) executes without an error,because printf("%d",a) statement and variable 'a' are in the same block .

Function Scope:

- The scope of a function start at the opening of the function({) and ends with closing of a function(}).
- The variable inside the function cannot give access to the outside.So, scope of such a variable is within that function.
- This variable can access anywhere in the function.
- When the function ends ,there the scope ends.

Example:

```
#include<stdio.h>
    void fun();
    main()
    {
    int x=10;
    printf("In main() %d",x);
    fun();
    }
    void fun();
    {
    printf("In fun %d",x);
    }
```

Explanation:

- In the above program the scope of the variable 'x' is upto end of the main function,but the programmer tried to access the variable 'x' from function fun().
- The variable 'x' in fun() throws an error because the scope of variable 'x' ends at main() function only.

File Scope:

> *"The variable which is declared outside the any function has file scope""*

- A variable which is declared outside the any function is known as global variable.The scope of that particular variable is throughtout the file.
- This variable can access anywhere in the program.
- Where the pogram ends , there the scope ends.

Example:

```
#include<stdio.h>
int x=10;
void fun();
main()
{
printf("In main():%d",x);
}
void fun()
{
printf("In fun():%d",x);
}
```

Explanation:

The variable 'x' value can be accessed throughout the program.

14. STORAGE CLASSES

> *""Storage class gives the information about variables to the compiler regarding storage area, lifetime, and default value.""*

There are 4 types of storage classes:

1. Automatic storage class.
2. External storage class.
3. Static storage class.
4. Register storage class.

Automatic Storage Class

- This is nothing but a local variable.
- A variable that is present inside any function or block by default is automatic storage class.
- It is not mandatory to declare a local variable with an auto keyword, implicitly the compiler adds an auto keyword before a local variable.

Important points about auto storage class:

- **Storage area:** The memory allocation for a variable with an auto keyword is done in the stack memory area.
- **Lifetime:** The lifetime of a variable with an auto keyword is up to the end of the block or a function.
- **Scope:** The scope of a variable with an auto keyword is within the function or block (local).
- **Default value:** The default value of a variable with an auto keyword is garbage.

Syntax:-

```
auto datatype variable_name;
```

Example:-

```
#include<stdio.h>
int main()
{
auto int p=29; //Declare a variable with auto
int s=24;//By default the compiler adds auto keyword
}
```

Explanation:-

In the above program

- Declare a variable with an auto keyword, i. e. auto int p=29 that is nothing but a local variable.
- Here there is another local variable without an auto keyword i. e., int s=24.
- But by default compiler adds auto keyword after the variable looks like auto int s=24

External Storage Class

- This is nothing but a global variable.
- A variable that is present outside any function or above the main() function by default is considered as an external storage class.
- It is not mandatory to declare a global variable with an extern keyword, implicitly the compiler adds the "extern" keyword before a global variable.

Important points about the extern storage class :

- **Storage area:** The memory allocation for a variable with an extern keyword is done at the data segment.
- Here we have 2 types of data segments in memory
- **Initialized data segment:** Initialized data segment means, it stores a global variable that is initialized by the programmer.
- **Uninitialized data segment:** Uninitialized data segment means, it stores a global variable that is initialized with 0(zero) by the kernel i. e. a global variable that is not initialized by the programmer the kernel initializer with 0(zero).
- **Lifetime:** The lifetime of a variable with the extern keyword is up to the end of the program.
- **Scope**: The scope of a variable with an extern keyword is throughout the program (global scope).
- **Default value:** The default value of a variable with an extern keyword is zero, it is initialized by the kernel.

Syntax:

extern int variable_name;

Example:-

```
#include<stdio.h>
extern int p=40;
int s;
int main()
{
printf("Value of global variable p is %d\n", p);
printf("Value of global variable s is %d\n", s);
}
```

Output:

The value of global variable p is 40

Value of global variable s is 0

Explanation:

In the above program

1. Declare a variable with extern keyword, i. e. extern int p=40; that is nothing but global variable.
2. Here there is another global variable without an extern keyword, i. e. int s.
3. In main() function we have 2 print statement, the 1st statement prints "value of global variable p is 40". And 2nd statement prints "value of global variable s is 0". Here the default value of global variable is zero.

Static Storage Class

- A variable which is declared with a static keyword is known as static variable.
- Static variable initializes only once, and it cannot re-initialize again and again, and it stores previously modified value.
- If we declare a local variable with static keyword it cannot loose the values in function calls, use normal variables

Important points about a Static Storage Class:

- **Storage Area:** The memory allocation for a variable with a static keyword done at data segment.
- **Lifetime:** The lifetime of a variable with static variable is up to end of the program.
- **Scope:** The scope of variable with static keyword is within the block of the function.
- **Default value:** The default value of a variable with static keyword is 0(zero).

Syntax:-
static data type variable_name;

Example:-

```
#include<stdio.h>
void fun_call();
void main()
{
int p;
for(p=1;p<=3;p++)
{
fun_call();
}
}
void fun_call()
{
int w=48;
static int d=24, k=29;
printf("d=%d\t k=%d\t w=%d\n", d, k, w);
d=d+1;
k=k+1;
w=w+1;
}
```

Output:-

d=24 k=29 w=48
d=25 k=30 w=48
d=26 k=31 w=48

Explanation:

In the above program

1. In the main() function, we have a for loop which iterates 3 times and along with that calling function i. e. fun_call, calls function definition 3 times.
2. For loop iteration:

For loop iteration 1:

- Inside for loop, we have calling function, that calls function definition.
- In the function definition normal variable w is initialized with 48, static variables d and k are initialized with 24 and 29 respectively. And print statement prints 'd=24 k=29 w=48' and after above statement is executed next variable d, k and w are incremented by 1. And now d, k and w holds 25, 30 and 49 respectively and after this control returns to the calling function.

For loop iteration 2:

- Again calling function calls function definition.
- In function main definition normal variable w is initialized with 48, but here variables d and k are static variables so it cannot re initialize again to 24 and 29 respectively now variables d and k stores previously updated value 25 and 30 respectively and print statement prints "d=25 k=30 w=48" and after this statement variables d, k and w is incremented by 1 and now d, k and w holds 26, 31 and 49 respectively and after this control returns to calling function.

For loop iteration 3:

- Again the calling function calls function definition.
- In the function definition normal variable reinitialize with 48, static variables d and k are dose not reinitialize again, it stores previously updated values 26 and 31 respectively and print statement prints "d=26 k=31 w=48" and after this control returns to the calling function.

Note:

1. Whenever a normal variable evaluated by the compiler, it is reinitialized with new value.
2. Whenever a static variable evaluated by the compiler, it never reinitializes with new values and it stores previously updated value only.

Register Storage Class

- A variable which is declared with register keyword is known as register variable.
- The register variable stores the assigned value at CPU registers instead of RAM. (Random Access Memory)
- Whenever register variable evaluates then the compiler checks that, is there any free register to register variable.
- If the compiler founds any free CPU register, then the compiler allocates free register to register variable.
- If the compiler cannot find any free CPU register, then the compiler allocates memory in RAM instead of CPU registers.

Advantages:

- Register variable gives better running time when compared to normal variables, because CPU registers are near to the CPU when compared to RAM.
- There is no address to CPU registers, it is impossible to access the data in CPU registers using pointers.

Important points about register storage class:

- **Storage Area:** The memory allocation for a variable with register keyword done at CPU registers.
- **Lifetime:** The lifetime of a variable with register keyword is up to end of the block or a function.
- **Scope:** The scope of a variable with register keyword is within the function or block(local).

- **Default value:** The default value of a variable with register keyword is garbage.

  Syntax:-

  register datatype variable_name;

  Example:-

```
#include<stdio.h>
void main()
{
register int d=24, k=29;
printf("Sum is :%d", d+k);
}
```

  Output:-

  Sum is:53

Explanation:

In the above program

1. Declare and initialize register variables, i. e. register int d=24, k=29.

- For above variables the memory allocates at CPU register.

2. The print statements prints "Sum is : 53" on the screen.

15. TYPE QUALIFIERS IN C :

Here we have mainly 2 types of qualifiers :

1. Volatile qualifier
2. Const qualifier

1. Volatile qualifier:

The volatile keyword is nothing but a qualifier which is used to declare along with a variable by programmer .

Syntax:

```
volatile int var_name;
int volatile var_name;
```

- The main use of volatile keyword is it is used to prevent optimization on our object.
- The object declared with volatile keword are executed from optimization because the values can be changed by outside of the code.
- If we try to access normal variable value, 1st time it will fetch from main memory and stores the value in intermediate memory like registers.
- If we try to acces again 2nd time the same variable,the control goes to intermediate memory i.e; registers to fetch the data rather than main memory.
- In case of volatile the control goes to main memory to fetch the data every time instead of intermediate memory i.e; registers

Case study:

Not declared global variable as volatile:

- In case of this ,2 threads are simultaneously updating the values in a global variable.
- If you want to access the previous value of that particular global variable , the control gives the values stored in the intermediate memory instead of main memory.
- The result will be wrong because 2 threads are updating the variable data continuously without any action being taken by the code.

Declare Global Variable as Volatile:

If we declare global variable as a volatile the control brings a variable data from main memory instead of intermediate memory to avoid interrupts.

Note: Volatile means always read data from main memory instead of intermediate memory like registers-No optimization is possible here.

```
int volatile x=10;
main ()
{
printf("%d",x);
}
```

2. Constant Qualifier:

A variable declared with a const keyword whose value can't be updated or altered.

Whenever a variable is prefixed with a constant keyword, the value in that variable is can't be modified once they defined

Syntax:

const datatype variable_name = value;

* Constant variable must be of any type like int, float, char...etc

* Constant value must be assigned at the time of constant variable declared.

const int pi=3.14

Example program :

```
main()
   {
   const int a = 24;
   int b=29;
   printf("%d",a+b);
   }
```

In the above program variable 'a' is declared as a constant.

Example program :

```
main()
{
const float x=24.29;
print ("%f",x);
x = 24.48; // update the constant value.
print f ("%f",x);
}
```

In the above program variable 'X' is declared as a floating-point constant with a value of 24.29. And very next the program changes the constant value from 24.29 to 24.48. Then the compiler sends an error saying that error: assignment of read-only variable X = 24.48

16. BASIC STRUCTURE OF THE C PROGRAM :

Documention Section [Comments]	/* Program Name : Sample Program Created by : T. Koti Mani Kumar Created On : 06/5/2022 */
Link Section	#include<stdio.h>
Definition Section	#define pi 3.14
Global declaration Section	int area_circle(); int r = 7;

Main() function section
{
Declaration part
Executable part
}
	void main()
	{
	Float area;
	area = area_circle();
	printf("Area of the circle is : %f ", area);
	}

Sub program section
[user-defined section]
Function1()
Function2()
.
.
Functionn()
	int area_circle()
	{
	return pi*r*r;
	}

Table 1.3 Basic Structure of the C program

Documentation Section :

This is nothing but a comment section. It is good practice to use the comment section above the program.

In C programming, we have 2 types of comments,

a. Single line comment
b. Multiple-line comment

At the time of execution, the compiler ignores the lines of code between ***comments.***

a. Single Line Comment : Use two slashes (//) to make a single-line comment.

Example:

```
#include<stdio. h>
void main ()
{
//print name and address
printf ("my name is Koti Mani Kumar from Amalapuram");
}
```

b. Multiple-Line Comment: Use a slash followed by an asterisk (/*) is for opening a multi-line comment and an asterisk followed by a slash (*/) is for closing a multi-line comment.

Syntax

```
/*
Line 1
Line 2
Line 3
*/
```

Example:

```
/*
Program Name: Sample program
Created by: T. Koti
Created on: 06/09/2020
*/
void main ()
{
printf ("my name is koti Mani kumar ");
}
```

B. Link Section

The link section gives instructions to the compiler to link the functions from the header files and this link section contains header files like #include

<stdio. h>, #include <math. h>.

Example:

```
#include <stdio. h>
#include <math. h>
```

C. Definition Section

Here #define is the preprocessor directive used to create constants. This section is used to declare macros. This is nothing but a symbolic constant.

Syntax: #define Identifier value;

Example:

```
#define pi 3.14
```

This is used to define constant values once you declare and assign a value, it is impossible to change.

D. Global Declaration Section

The global declaration section is the place where to declare global variables, which can access throughout the program, and is also to declare a function prototype.

Example:

```
int area_ circle (); //function prototype
int r=7; //global variable;
main ()
[
//statements;
]
```

E. main() Function Section

It is a very important section. It has 2 parts

- **Declaration Part**

The declaration part is used to declare local variables and constant variables.

- **Executable Part**

The executable part must contain at least one statement. This part may contain statements like print, calculation part etc...

Both declaration and executable parts are present inside brace '{'and ends with a closing brace '}'.

F. Sub Program Section

This is the place where all user-defined functions are defined. All these user-defined functions are called from the main () function.

Example:

```
int area_circle ()
{
return pi*r*r;
}
```

17. ASSOCIATIVITY AND PRECEDENCE:

Associativity:

Associativity means in an expression contains operators with the same priority or precedence then based on their associated CPU decides the order in which they execute

X= 6/3 + 1 * 55 % 10

In the above expression *, / and % have precedence with associativity left to right

Hence / (divide by) executes 1st , *(multiplication) executes 2nd and % (modulus) will executes last.

X = 6/3 + 3 * 55 % 10

//CPU gives 1st priority to '/'

X= 3 + 1 * 55 % 10

//Next CPUgives 2nd priority to multiplication

X = 3 + 55 % 10

//Next CPU gives 3rd priority to modulus

X = 3 +5

//Next do addition

X = 8

Precedence :

The C language has some protocols to give priority to operators

That protocol or rule is known as operator precedence

The CPU executes total expression operator by operator as per their precedence

In C the rank of arithmetic operators (*, %, / , +, -) is higher than relational operator (==,!=,>,<,<=,>=) relational operators is higher than logical operators (&&,|| and !)

Example on precedence :

X = 29 +(13 -7) * 24

//CPU gives 1st priority to brackets ( )

X = 29 + 6 * 24

//CPU gives priority to * (Multiplication)

X = 29 + 144

//Next do addition

X= 173

18. TYPE CONVERSION STATEMENTS

Type Conversions and Casting

"Type conversion converts one data type to another data type."

- Type conversion means system converts low rank data type to high rank data type without any data loss.
- Type casting means developer/programmer needs to convert explicitly. from high rank data type to low rank data type.
- In this C programming come up with 2 types of type conversions.

  i. Implicit type conversion
  ii. Explicit type conversion

Implicit Type Conversion

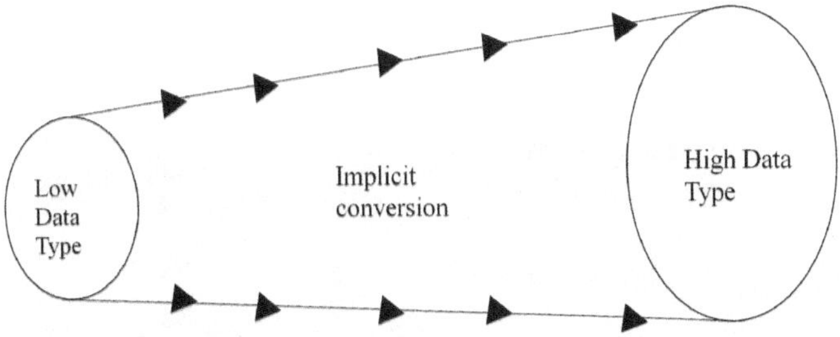

Figure 1.10 Implicit Conversion

In C programming system or compiler converts low rank data type to high rank data type without any casting is known as Implicit type conversion (or) automatic type conversion.

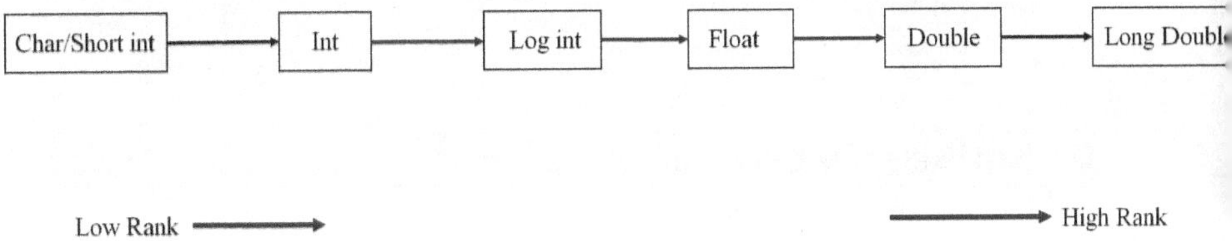

Figure 1.11 Data types low to high rank

Example: In the following example, converting integer number to floating point numbers.

Program:

```
#include <stdio.h>
int main()
{
int a=20;
float b=a; // implicit conversion
printf("After implicit conversion:%f", b);
}
```

Output: After implicit conversion:20.000000

Explanation:

In the above example

1. Variable **int a** is declared.
2. Variable **float b** is declared.
3. **float b = a;** here **int** is converted into **float.** This type of conversion is called automatic type conversion. Here the result is 20.000000

Case Study on Implicit Conversion

Case-1: long double =long double + int

Program:

```
#include <stdio.h>
int main()
{
long double a=29.890;
int b=24;
long double c=a+b; //implicit conversion
printf("Value of c is:%Lf", c);
return 0;
}
```

Output: Value of c is:53.890000

Explanation:

In the above program has an expression **long double c=a + b**

Here operand "a" [type-long double] is the high rank data type and corresponding operand "b" [type-int] is the low rank data type. So, the compiler automatically converts low rank data type to high rank data type. Then "int" data type is implicitly converted to long double so, that result occurred in long double i.e. 29.890000+24.000000 = 53.890000

Note: If any one of the operands is with high rank data type, then remaining low rank data types automatically get promoted to high rank data type and the result will get in high rank data type present in that expression.

Case-2:float =float + int

```
#include <stdio.h>
int main()
```

```
{
float a=29.48;
int b=24;
float c=a+b;
printf("Value of c is:%f", c);
}
```

Output: Value of c is:53.480000

Explanation:

In the above program has an expression **float c = a + b** here operand "a" [type-float] is the high rank data type and corresponding operand "b" [type-int] is the low rank data type. So, the compiler automatically converts low rank data type to high rank data type. Then "int" data type is automatically converted to "float".

So that result occurred in float, i.e. 29. 48+24. 000000=53.4

Case-3: double = double +int

```
#include <stdio.h>
int main()
{
double a=29.11;
int b=24;
double c=a+b;
printf("Value of c:% lf", c);
}
```

Output: Value of c: 53.110000

Explanation:

In the above program has an expression **double c=a + b** here operand "a" [type-double] is the high rank data type and corresponding operand "b" [type-int] is the low rank data type. So, the compiler automatically coverts low rank data type to high rank data type. Then "int" data type is automatically converted to double. So that result occurred in double, i.e. 29.11+24.00= 53.110000

Case-4: int = int +char

```
#include <stdio.h>
int main()
{
int a=13;
```

```
char b='d'; //ASCII value of'd' is 100
int c=a+b;
printf("Value of c:%d", c);
return 0;
]
```

Output:Value of c:113

Explanation:

In the above program has an expression **int c=a + b** here operand "a" [type-int] is the high rank data type and corresponding operand "b" [type-char] is the low rank data type. So, the compiler automatically converts low rank data type high rank data type. Then "**char**" data type is automatically converted to "**int**" data type. ASCII value for "d" is 100. So that result occurred in "**int**" i.e. 13+100 = 113.

Explicit Type Conversion

Explicit type conversion means programmer/developer needs to convert high rank data type to the low rank data type explicitly.

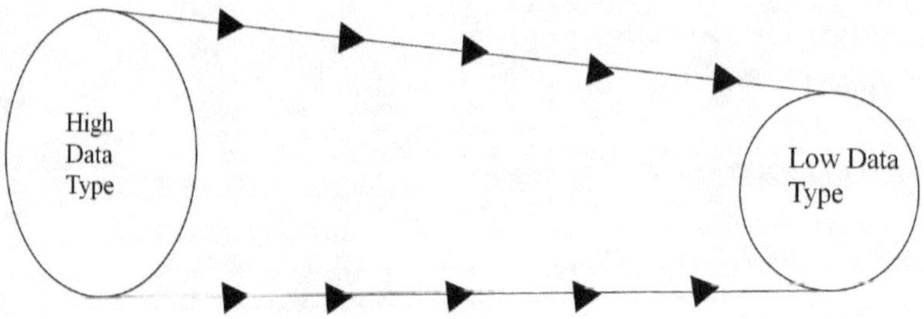

Figure 1.12 Explicit type conversion

Syntax: *(data_type) expression;*

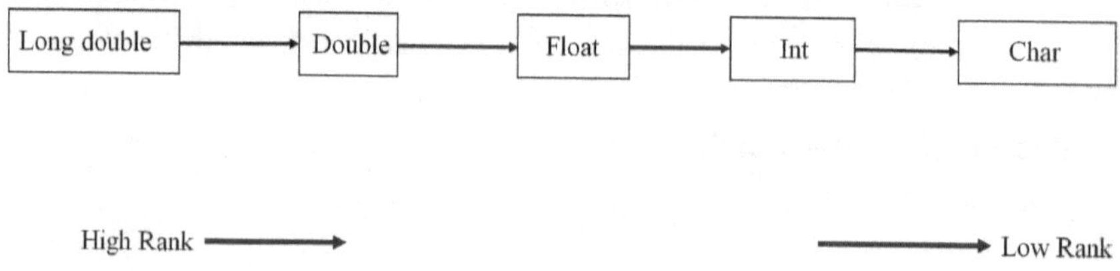

Figure 1.13 Data types high rank to low rank

Example:

float a = 24.29;
int b;
b = (int) a;

Program:

In the following example, converting float to int (explicit type casting)

```
#include <stdio.h>
int main()
{
float a=24.29;
int b=(int)a;
printf("After explicit conversion:%d", b);
return 0;
}
```

Output: After explicit conversion:24

Explanation:

In the above program has expressed **int b = (int)a;** here operand "a" [type-float] is the high rank data type and another operand "b"[type-int] is the low rank data type. So, here high rank data type [float] is converted to low rank data type [int], due to this compiler does not convert automatically. So, a programmer / developer needs to type cast to "int" , i.e., (int) a.

Case Study on Explicit Conversion

Case-1: float c = (float)a/b;

```
#include <stdio.h>
int main()
{
float c;
int a=29, b=24;
c=(float)a/b;
printf("value of c: %f", c);
return 0;
}
```

Output: value of c: 1.208333

Explanation:

In the above program hasexpression **c = (float) a/b**; firstly operand 'a' [type-int] is divided by operand 'b'[type-int] and at the same time operand 'a' is explicitly converted to **"float"** and the above statement operand 'a' is **"float"** and operand "b" is promoted from "int" to "float" [Rule: float/intàfloat] and the result is in "float" i.e. 29.000000/24.000000 = 1.208333

Case-2: float c = (float)(a/b)

```
#include <stdio.h>
int main()
[
float c;
int a=29, b=24;
c=(float)(a/b);
printf("Value of c: %f", c);
return 0;
]
```

Output: Value of c: 1.000000

Explanation:

In the above program has expression **c = (float) (a/b)** firstly operand 'a' [type-int] is divided by operand 'b' [type-int] the result is in integer, i.e. (29/24) = 1 (int/intèint) then the result is 1.In the above statement first a/b is evaluated and then the result is explicitly converted to **"float"** then it becomes 1.000000 and assigned to operand 'c' [type-float].

Note: float c = (float) a/b; is totally different from **float c = (float) (a/b).**

19. COMMAND LINE ARGUMENTS :

The arguments / parameter passed through command line is called command line arguments

A main( ) function has two parameters, those parameters are passed by Value through the command line, and 1st argument is used to count the number of arguments passed through the command line i.e, argc and 2nd argument is a pointer array, that points to every argument passed through command line

Syntax :

```
int main ( int argc,char *argv[ ])
{
//Statement ;
}
```

argc:

It is an integer type.

It is used to store the count of the parameters passed through Command-line.

It cant be a negative value.

argv[ ]:

It is a pointer array, that points to every argument passed through the command line.

Example:

```
#include <stdio.h>
main( int argc,char *argv[ ])
{
int x;
if (argc >= 2)
{
printf("Argument values ");
for (x=1;x < argc;x++)
{
printf("%s",argv[ x ] );
}
}
else
{
printf("List is Empty ");
}
}
```

Explanation :

Pass the parameters like $./a.out sample prog 24 29 cherry.

Here there are 5 items on command line, so argc = 5.

argv[0] = “sample prog”
argv[1] = “ 24 “
argv[2] = “29 “
argv[3] =” cherry”

II

OPERATORS, MAKING DECISIONS & REPETITION

CONTENTS : Exact Size Integer Types, Operators. Selection & Making Decisions: Two Way Selection, Multiway Selection, Intialisation and updating, More Standard Functions. Repetition: Concept of Loop, Pretest and Post-test Loops,, Other Statements Related to Looping, Looping Applications, Programming Examples.

1. EXACT SIZE INTEGERS TYPES :

The size of the integer is system dependent

In 32 bit system, the size of the integer is 2 bytes whereas in the 64-bit system the size of the integer is 4 bytes

All the integer types are the exact or fixed size which means they are represented in the form of fixed number b and cannot be expanded beyond the range

In C language has permission to define integer types of size 8,16, 32, and 64 bits

All these are works under the stdint.h header file

Here we have two types of integer

1. Signed integer
2. Unsigned integer

Signed Integer :

It represents either positive or negative numbers

Type Name Meaning
int 8_t It is 1 byte signed integer
int 16_t It is 2 byte signed integer
int 32_t It is 4 byte signed integer
int 64_t It is 8 byte signed integer
int ptr_t It is signed integer of size equal to a pointer

Unsigned Integer:

It is an integer data type that can store zero to positive numbers.

Type Name Meaning
uint 8_t It is 1 byte unsigned integer
uint 16_t It is 2 byte unsigned integer
uint 32_t It is 4 byte unsigned integer
uint 64_t It is 8 byte unsigned integer
uint ptr_t It is an unsigned integer of size equal to a pointer

A C-program to illustrate about signed and unsigned integer

```
#include<stdio.h>
#include<stdint.h>
main()
{
//Signed Integer
int8_t a1 = -24;
int16_t b1 = -129;
int32_t c1 = -2429;
int64_t d1 = -24292;
//Unsigned Integer
uint8_t a2 = 24;
uint16_t b2 = 129;
uint32_t c2 = 2429;
uint64_t d2 = 24292;
printf("Size of int8_t :%d \n Size of int16_t :%d \n Size of int32_t :%d \n
Size of int64_t :%d \n",sizeof(a1), sizeof(b1), sizeof(c1), sizeof(d1));
```

```
printf("Size of uint8_t :%d \n Size of uint16_t :%d \n Size of uint32_t :%d
\n Size of uint64_t :%d \n",sizeof(a2), sizeof(b2), sizeof(c2), sizeof(d2));
}
```

2. OPERATORS

"The operators are used to perform an operation on operands."

C language can provide the following types of operators.

1. Arithmetic operators
2. Bitwise operators
3. Assignment operators
4. Special operators
5. Increment/Decrement operators
6. Relational operators
7. Conditional operators
8. Logical operators

Arithmetic Operators

Here the basic arithmetic operators are Addition (+), Subtraction (-), Multiplication (*), Division (/), Modulus (%).

- Here Addition operator is used to adding the values of left and right operands.
- Subtraction operator is used to subtract the values of left and right operands.
- Multiplication operator is used to multiply the values of left and right operands.
- Division operator is used to divide left operand with the right operand.
- Modulus operator is used to divide the operands and return remainder.

Operators	Meaning	Example (int d=29, p=24)
+(Addition)	Used to add left and right operand values	d+p
- (Subtraction)	Used to subtract left and right operand values	d-p
* (Multiplication)	Used to multiple by left and right operand values	d*p
/(Division)	Used to divide two operands and gives quotient values as a resul	d/p
% (Module)	It gives remainder as a result	d%p

Table 2.1 Arithmetic Operators

An example program to illustrate an Arithmetic Operators

```
#include<stdio.h>
void main()
{
int d=29, p=24;
printf("Addition is %d\n", d+p);
printf("Subtraction is %d\n", d-p);
printf("Multiplication is %d\n", d*p);
printf("Division is %d\n", d/p);
printf("Module is %d\n", d%p);
}
```

Output:

Addition is 53
Subtraction is 5
Multiplication is 696
Division is 1
Module is 5

Explanation:

In the above program

1. Declare two operands /variables that 'd' and 'p' with 29 and 24 respectively.
2. Next perform addition using '+' operator on two operands d and p and output is printed on screen.
3. Next perform subtraction using '-' operator on two operands d and p and output is printed on screen.
4. Next perform multiplication using '*' operator on two operands d and p and output is printed on screen.
5. Next perform division using '/' operator on two operands d and p is divisor and display quotient as output on screen.
6. Next perform division using '%' operator on two operands d and p is divisor and Display remainder as output on screen.

Bitwise Operators

Bitwise operator means it should perform operation on bits but not on values.

For example if we perform bitwise AND (&) operation on two operands then the system converts those two operand values into binary form (bits) , then bitwise AND operation is performed, and same for bitwise OR (|), bitwise XOR (^), bitwise compliment(~), left shift (<<) and right shift (>>).

In Bitwise the arithmetic operators like addition, subtraction, and division are done at bit-level.
The C language provides different bitwise operators like Bitwise AND (&), Bitwise OR (|), Bitwise XOR(^), Bitwise compliment(~), Left shift(<<), and Right shift(>>).

The following table lists the **Bitwise** operators

Operators	Meaning	Example
&	Bitwise AND	int d=24, p=29; d&p -> 24
|	Bitwise OR	int d=24, p=29, d|p -> 29
^	Bitwise XOR	int d=9, p=10, d^p -> 3
~	Bitwise compliment	int d=24, ~ d -> 231
<<	Left shift	int p=10 p<1=4
>>	Right shift	int p=10 p>>1=5

Table 2.2 Bitwise Operators

Bitwise AND(&)

The result of Bitwise AND (&) is true, when the bit of left operand and corresponding bit of right operand is true.

1. This operator performs bitwise AND operation on corresponding bits of an operands.

- let us take two variables

int d=24, p=29;

- Perform bitwise AND on above operands d and p, i.e., d&p

Note : Complier convert value in variable d, i.e., 24 to binary And also converts the value in variable p, i.e 29 to binary and then bitwise AND operation performed on corresponding bits.

d=24 = 0 0 0 1 1 0 0 0
p=29 = 0 0 0 1 1 1 0 1

----

d & p = 0 0 0 1 1 0 0 0

----

d & p = $(00011000)_2$ =24

- Output of d & p is 24

Bitwise OR(|)

- This operator performs bitwise OR(|) operation on corresponding bits of an operands.
- Bitwise OR(|) gives true, when any one of the corresponding bits of two operands are true.

i. let us take two variables

int d=24, p=29;

i. Perform bitwise OR on above operands d and p, i.e, d | p

d=24 = 0 0 0 1 1 0 0 0
p=29 = 0 0 0 1 1 1 0 1

----

d | p = 0 0 0 1 1 1 0 1

----

d | p $(00011101)_2$ =29
Output of d | p is 29

Bitwise XOR (^)

If bitwise XOR(^) gives true , when the bit of left operand is true and the corresponding bit of the right operand must be false or when the bit of left operand is false and the corresponding bit of the right operand must be true.

let us take two variables
int d=9, p=10;
Perform bitwise XOR on above operands d and p, i.e, d ^ p
d=9 à 0 0 0 0 1 0 0 1
p=10 à 0 0 0 0 1 0 1 0

----

d ^ p à 0 0 0 0 0 0 1 1

----

d ^ p à $(00000011)_2$ =3
Output of d & p is 3

Bitwise Compliment(~)

It is also called one's complement operator or bitwise operator.
It donated by tilde operator (~).
Take a variable
int d=24;
Apply tilde (~) operator to above variable 'd'
d=24=>0 0 0 1 1 0 0 0
~d = 1 1 1 0 0 1 1 1
~d = $(1\,1\,1\,0\,0\,1\,1\,1)_2$ =231

- Output of ~d is 231

Shift Operators :

Left Shift (<<)

Shift operator removes the specific number of bits at MSB(Most Significant Bits) and adds removed number of 0 bits at LSB(Least Significant Bits) or other side.

Syntax:
Operand << N

- First the value in operand converts into binary form
- Remove' N number of bits at MSB and add 'N' number of 0 bits at LSB.

Example 1 :
int p=10;
0000 1010 << 1
After left shift by 1 the result is 0001 0100
The output of p<<1 is 20.
Example 2 :
int p=10;
0000 1010 << 2

After left shift by 2 the result is 0010 1000

The output of p<<2 is 40.

Right Shift (>>):

Right Shift operator removes the specified number of bits at MSB(Most Significant Bits) and adds removed number of 0 bits at LSB (Least Significant Bits) or other side.

Syntax:

Operand >> N

- First the value in operand converts into binary form
- Remove' N number of bits at MSB and add 'N' number of 0 bits at LSB.

Example 1:

int p=10;

0000 1010 >> 1

After right shift by 1 the result is **0000 0101**

The output of p>>1 is 5 .

Example 2:

int p=10;

1010 >> 2

After right shift by 2 the result is 0000 **0010**

The output of p>>2 is 2.

An Example program to illustrate bitwise Operators.

```
#include<stdio.h>
void main()
{
int d=24, p=29;
printf ("Bitwise AND: %d\n", d &p);
printf ("Bitwise OR : %d\n", d | p);
d=9, p=10;
printf ("Bitwise XOR : %d\n", d ^ p);
d=24;
printf ("Bitwise complement: %d\n", ~d);
p=10;
printf ("Left shift: %d\n", p<<1);
printf ("Right shift : %d\n", p>>1);
}
```

Output:
Bitwise AND: 24
Bitwise OR : 29
Bitwise XOR : 3
Bitwise complement: -25
Left shift: 20
Right shift : 5

Explanation:

In the above program In the above program prints the values of bitwise AND, bitwise OR , bitwise XOR, bitwise compliment, left shift and right shift.

Assignment Operators :

By using assignment operator, values for variables are assigned i.e. right side value of equal to operator assigns to left side variable.

The following table lists the assignment operators.

Operator	Description	Example
=	Assigns left side value to the right side	int d =24;
+=	It adds left side value to the value in the right side variable a assign the return to right side variable	int d=24; int d+=5; i.e. d=d+5;
-=	It subtracts left side value to the value in the right side variable a assign the return to right side variable	int d=24; int d-=5; i.e. d=d-5;
*=	It multiplies left side value to the value in the right side variable a assign the return to right side variable	int d=24; int d*=5; i.e. d=d*5;
/=	It divides left side value to the value in the right side variable a assign the return to right side variable	int d=24; int d/=5; i.e. d=d/5;
%=	It divides left side value to the value in the right side variable a assign the remainder to right side variable	int d=24; int d%=5; i.e. d=d %5;

Table 2.3 Assignment Operators

An example program to illustrate Assignment Operators.

```
#include <stdio.h>
void main()
{
int d=24; //Assignment operator
printf("Result of d+=5 is %d\n", d+=5);
printf("Result of d-=5 is %d\n", d-=5);
printf("Result of d*=5 is %d\n", d*=5);
printf("Result of d/=5 is %d\n", d/=5);
printf("Result of d%=5 is %d\n", d%=5);
}
```

Output:

Result of d+=5 is 29
Result of d-=5 is 24
Result of d*=5 is 120
Result of d/=5 is 24
Result of d%=5 is 4

Explanation:

In the above program

1. The value 24 assigns to variable d.
2. Next statement prints the value of d+=5 i.e. d=d+5 the output is "Result of d+=5 is 29".
3. Next statement prints the value of d-=5 i.e. d=d-5 the output is "Result of d-=5 is 24".
4. Next statement prints the value of d*=5 i.e. d=d*5 the output is "Result of d*=5 is 120".
5. Next statement prints the value of d/=5 i.e. d=d/5 the output is "Result of d/=5 is 24".
6. Next statement prints the value of d%=5 i.e. d=d%5 the output is "Result of d%=5 is 4".

Special Operators :

An example program to illustrate a Special Operators.

Operator	Description	Example
&	It is used to fetch the address of a variable	int p; printf("%u", &p);
*	It is used as a pointer to a variable.	int *p;

,	When multiple values are separated with comma operator within the braces, then the value which is right most to the comma considered as the result of the expression.	if(0, 24)
		{
		printf("true");
		}
		else
		{
		printf("false");
		}

sizeof()	It is used to fetch the size of the variable.	int p; printf("%d", sizeof(p));

Table 2.4 Special operators

Program:

```
#include <stdio.h>
void main()
[
int d=24;
int p; // is a special operator
p = &d; //& is a special operator
if(0, 24)//comma is a special operator
[
printf("True\n");
]
else
[
printf("False\n");
]
printf("Size of variable d is %d", sizeof(d));//sizeof is a special operator
```

}

Output:

True

Size of variable d is 4

Explanation:

In the above program

1. * is a special operator pointer to a variable p.

2. & is a special operator, which is used to fetch the address of the a variable d.

3. Comma is a special operator, the value of right most of the comma is 24 then if condition returns true and control enters in the body of the if and prints "true" on to screen.

Increment or Decrement Operators :

Increment operator:

Here we have two types of increment operations,

1. Pre increment:

The pre increment increments the value in the variable immediately.

Syntax:

++ variable_name;

2. Post increment:

The post increment increments the value in the variable at the time of evaluation, it increment the value whenever the control goes to next instruction.

Syntax:

Variable _name + +;

2. Post decrement operator:

The post decrement does not decrement the value in the variable at the time of evaluation of the decrement statement, it decrement the value in the variable whenever the control goes to the next instruction.

Syntax:

Variable_name - -;

An example program to illustrate increment and decrement operator.

```
#include <stdio.h>
void main()
{
int d=24;
```

```
printf("Value of d is:%d\n", d);
printf("Pre increment of d is:%d\n", ++d);
printf("Value of d after pre increment is:%d\n", d);
printf("Post increment of d is:%d\n", d++);
printf("Value of d after post increment is:%d\n", d);
printf("Pre decrement of d is:%d\n", --d);
printf("Value of d after pre decrement is:%d\n", d);
printf("Post decrement of d is:%d\n", d--);
printf("Value of d after post decrement is:%d\n", d);
}
```

Output:

Value of d is:24
Pre increment of d is:25
Value of d after pre increment is:25
Post increment of d is:25
Value of d after post increment is:26
Pre decrement of d is:25
Value of d after pre decrement is:25
Post decrement of d is:25
Value of d after post decrement is:24

Explanation:

In the above program, shows pre and post increment and decrement operations on variable d.

Relational Operators :

Relational operators used to compare the values of two operand or expression. These operators gives the result in boolean form , i.e. 1 for true and 0 for false.

The following table lists the relational operators

Operator	Meaning	Example
< (Less than)	Result is true, when left operand value is less than right operand value	d<p
>(greater than)	Result is true, when left operand value is greater than right operand value	d>p
<= (Less than or equal to)	Result is true, when left operand value is less than or equal to right operand value	d<=p
>=(greater than or equal to)	Result is true, when left operand value is greater than or equal to right operand value	d>=p
= =(equal to)	Result is true, when left operand value is equal to right operand value	d= =p
!=(not equal to)	Result is true, when left operand value is not equal to right operand value	d!=p

Table 2.5 Relational Operators

An example program to illustrate Relational Operators

```
#include<stdio.h>
void main()
{
int d=29, p=24;
printf("value in d is < value in p: %d", d<p);
printf("value in d is > value in p: %d", d<p);
printf("value in d is <= value in p: %d", d<=p);
printf("value in d is >=value in p: %d", d>=p);
printf("value in d is = = value in p: %d", d= =p);
printf("value in d is != value in p: %d", d!=p);
}
```

Output:

value in d is < value in p: 0

value in d is > value in p: 1

value in d is <= value in p: 0

value in d is >=value in p: 1

value in d is = = value in p: 0

value in d is != value in p: 1

Explanation:

In the above program

1.Declare two operands /variables that 'd' and 'p' with 29 and 24 respectively.

2. Next Compare using '<' operator on two operands d and p and output is printed on screen.

3. Next Compare using '>' operator on two operands d and p and output is printed on screen.

4. Next Compare using ' < =' operator on two operands d and p and output is printed on screen.

5. Next Compare using ' >=' operator on two operands d and p and output is printed on screen.

6. Next Compare using '= =' operator on two operands d and p and output is printed on screen.

7. Next Compare using '!=' operator on two operands d and p and output is printed on screen.

Conditional Operators:

This is also called ternary operator, i.e. it is mainly works on 3 operands that's why it is called ternary operator. It has 2 symbols one is "?" and another one is ":". The working of conditional operator is same as working of if else statement.The use of the conditional operator is to write if else statement in a single line, i.e. . it reduces the line of code.

Syntax:

Expression1? Expression 2: Expression 3;

Here expression 1 is test condition, if it is true; then the expression 2 will gets executed and otherwise expression 3 will get executed.

An example program to illustrate conditional or ternary operator.

```
#include <stdio.h>
void main()
{
int d=24;
(d%2==0)? printf("Even number"):printf("Odd number");
}
```

Output:

Even number

Explanation:

In the above program

1. Declare a variable d and initialize with value 24.
2. Next checks the condition (d%2==0) on the success the control executes the statement after the? Symbol and prints 'Even number".
3. On failure the control executes the statement after the ":" symbol and prints "Odd number".

Logical Operator :

Logical Operators are used to perform logical operations like &&, || and ! on operands or expression.

Here we have 3 operators

i. Logical AND (&&)

ii.Logical OR (||)

iii.Logical NOT(!)

i. Logical AND (&&)

If both the operands are true then only the result of logical AND is true, otherwise false.

p	d	P&&d
1	1	1
0	1	0
1	0	0
0	0	0

Logical AND (&&)

ii.Logical OR (||)

If both the operands are false, then only the result of logical OR is false, otherwise true.

p	d	p || d
1	1	1
0	1	1
1	0	1
0	0	0

Table 2.6 Logical OR (||)

Logical NOT(!):

If the operands is true then, the result of logical NOT is false.

p	!p
1	0
0	1

Table 2.7 Logical NOT(!):

An example program to illustrate the Logical Operators

```
#include<stdio.h>
void main()
{
int d=29, p=24, q=48, s=90;
printf( "logical AND: %d\n", ((d<p&&q<s)));
printf( "logical OR: %d\n", ((d<p||q<s)));
printf(" logical NOT: %d\n", !p);
}
```

Output:
logical AND: 0
logical OR: 1
logical NOT: 0
Explanation:
In the above program
1.Declare and initialize 4 variables d, p, q, and s with 24, 48 and 90 respectively.
2. After evaluate the statement (d<p)&&(q<s) it returns true or 1.
Evaluation process of the above statement, i.e., (d<p)&&(q<s) shown in below table:

d	p	q	s	d<p	q<s	(d<p)&&(q<s)
24	29	48	90	True	true	(True)&&(true)=(true)

Evaluation process of (d<p)&&(q<s)

3.After evaluate the statement (d<p)||(q<s) it returns true or 1.
Evaluation process of above statement, i.e., **(d<p)||(q<s)** shown in below table :

d	p	q	s	d<p	q<s	(d<p)||(q<s)
24	29	48	90	True	false	(True)||(false)=(true)

Evaluation process of (d<p)||(q<s)

4. After evaluating the statement !p, it returns 0 or false as output.

3. SELECTION AND MAKING DECISIONS

Introduction

"Selection and decisions making statements in c programming tells about the execution direction. If the condition is true, the control enters

into one block. Otherwise control enters into another block of statements."

The selection and decision-making statements in programming are:

One way selection :

- if Statement

Two way selection :

- if...else Statement

Multi way Selection :

- if-else-if Ladder
- Nested if Statement
- switch Statement
- Jump statement

One way Selection

if Statement

"It is one of the simple selections and decision making statements in c programming. If the condition is true, the control executes a block of statements otherwise not."

Syntax:-

```
if(condition)
{
//statements;
}
```

Flowchart :

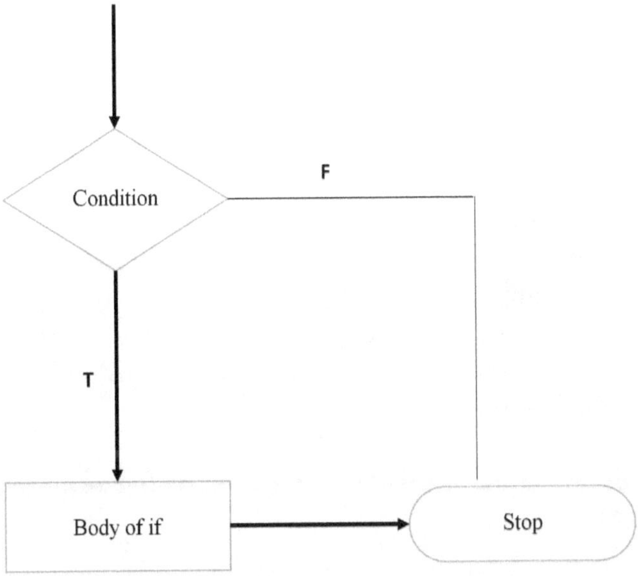

Figure 2.1 If statement

Explanation:-

If the condition is true, then the control enters into the 'body of the if' otherwise compiler ignores 'body of the if'.

Example Programs: -

1. Write a c program to print "positive", if the given number is greater than zero.

Program :

```
#include<stdio.h>
int main()
{
int num;
printf("Enter any number:"); scanf("%d", &num);
if(num>=0)
{
printf("\nPositive");
}
}
```

Output: -

Enter any number: 10

Positive

Explanation: -

In the above program

1. Declare a variable '**num**'.
2. Read the data from the keyboard using **scanf ()** and store the value in variable '**num**'.
3. Check the condition i.e. **if(num>=0)**, on success, control enters into the body of the **if** block and prints the output '**Positive**'.
4. On failure, terminate.

2. Ask user to enter integer 'k', if 24<=n<=29, then print number is in between 24 to 29.

Program: -

```
#include<stdio.h>
    int main()
    {
    int k;
    printf("Enter k value:");
    scanf("%d", &k);
    if(k>=24 && k<=29)
    {
    printf("\nNumber is in between 24 and 29");
    }
    }
```

Output: Enter k value: 26

Number is in between 24 and 29

Explanation: -

In the above program

1. Declare a variable '**k**'.
2. Read the data from the keyboard using **scanf ()** and store the value in variable '**k**'.
3. Check the condition, i.e. **if(k>=24 && k<=29)**, on success, control enters into the body of the **if** block and prints the output '**Number is in between 24 to 29** '.
4. On failure, terminate.

Two way selection :

if..else Statement

> *"In this statement, if the condition **true**, the control enters into the body of the **if** block, otherwise the control enters into the **else**block."*

Syntax: -

```
if(condition)
    {
    //body of the if
    }
    else
    {
    //body of the else
    }
```

Flowchart :

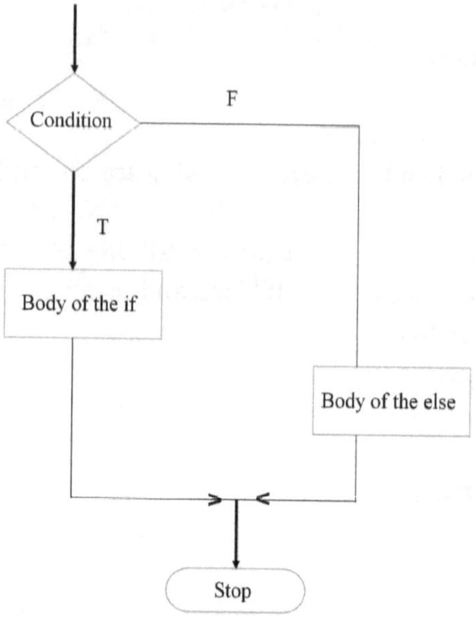

Figure 2.2 Flowchart of if...else

Example Programs: -

1. Ask user to enter integer "k" and check whether an integer is even or odd.

Program: -

```
#include<stdio.h>
int main()
{
int k;
printf("Enter k value:\n");
scanf("%d", &k);
if(k%2==0)
{
printf("It is an even number");
}
else{
printf("It is a odd number");
}
```

]

Output: -

Enter k value:10
It is an even number
Enter k value:1
It is a odd number

Explanation: -

In the above program

1. Declare a variable '**k**'.
2. Read the data from the keyboard using **scanf ()** and store the value in variable '**k**'.
3. Check the condition, i.e.**if(k%2==0)**, on success, control enters into the body of the **if** block and prints the output '**It is an even number**'.
4. On failure, the control enters into the body of the **else** block and prints "**It is a odd number**".

2. Ask user to enter 3 angles of a triangle, If the sum of 3 angles are equal to 180 and angles a1, a2 and a3 is not zero then print triangle is valid. Otherwise, print triangle is invalid.

Program: -

```
#include<stdio.h>
int main()
[
int a1, a2, a3, s=0;
printf("Enter 3 angles of triangle: \n");
scanf("%d %d %d", &a1, &a2, &a3);
s=a1+a2+a3;
if (s==180&&a1!=0&&a2!=0&&a3!=0)
[
printf("Triangle is valid");
]
else[
printf("Triangle is valid");
]
]
```

Output:

Enter 3 angles of triangle: 90 40 50
Triangle is valid

Explanation: -

In the above program

1. Declare the variables **a1, a2** and **a3** and **s=0.**
2. Read the data from the keyboard using **scanf ()**and store the values in variables a1, a2 and a3 respectively.
3. Do sum of 3 angles (**a1+a2+a3**) and store the result in variable '**s**'.
4. Check the condition i.e. if (s==180&&a1!=0&&a2!=0&&a3! =0), on success, control enters into the body of the **if** block and prints the output '**Triangle is valid**'.
5. On failure, the enters into the body of the **else** block and prints "**Triangle is invalid**".

3. A shopping mall conducts festival sale with discount on the amount you purchase, If purchased amount is greater than 5000 Rupees give 20% discount, otherwise give 5% discount. Write a C program to calculate the net amount after discount?

Program:-

```
#include <stdio.h>
int main()
{
double purchase_amt, discount, sale_price;
printf("Enter the purchased amount_:");
scanf("%lf", &purchase_amt);
if(purchase_amt>5000)
{
discount=(purchase_amt*20)/100;
}
else
{
discount=(purchase_amt*5)/100;
}
```

```
sale_price=purchase_amt - discount;
printf("Net amount after discount is_:%lf", sale_price);
}
```

Output: -

1. Enter the purchased amount_:5500
Net amount after discount is_:4400.000000
2. Enter the purchased amount_:3500
Net amount after discount is_:3325.000000

Explanation:-

In the above program

1. Declare variables **purchase_amount, discount, sale_price.**
2. Read the purchase amount from keyboard using **scanf ()** and stored in variable **purchase_amount.**
3. Check the condition, i.e. (**purchase_amount> 5000**), on success, the control enters into the body of the **if** block and calculate discount with **20%** on purchase amount, on failure, calculate the discount with **5%** on purchase amount.
4. Do difference between purchase_amount and discount and store the result in **sale_price** and finally Prints sale_price. i.e. **Net amount after discount.**

4. In a college there is rule to get a hostel seat for senior students is, the student must have above 80% attendance with less than 2 backlogs will get a seat in the hostel. Take the following inputs from user, there are number of classes held, number of classes attend, number of backlogs. Write a C program, Whether the student is eligible for hostel seat are not?

Program:-

```
#include <stdio.h>
int main()
{
int backlogs;
float classes_held, classes_attend, per;
printf("Enter total no. of classes held_:");
scanf("%f \n ", &classes_held);
printf("Enter total no. of classes attend_:");
```

```
scanf("%f\n", &classes_attend);
printf("Enter total no. of backlogs_:");
scanf("%d", &backlogs);
per=(classes_attend/classes_held)*100;
if(per>80 && backlogs<2)
{
printf("Congrats! You are eligible for hostel seat");
}
else
{
printf("Sorry! Better luck next time");
}
}
```

Output:-

```
Enter total no. of classes held_:500
Enter total no. of classes attend_:400
Enter total no. of backlogs_:5
Sorry! Better luck next time
Enter total number of classes_held_:500
Enter total no. of classes attend_:490
Enter total no. of backlogs_:1
Congrats! You are eligible for hostel seat
```

Explanation: -

In the above program,

1. Declare the variables **backlogs, classes_held, classes_attend, percent.**
2. Read the data from the keyboard using **scanf()**and stored in **classes_held, classes_attend** and **backlogs.**
3. Divide 'classes_attend' with 'classes_held'and multiply with hundred and store the result in a variable '**percent**'.
4. Check the condition, i.e. **if (per>80&& backlogs<2)**, On success the control enters into the body of the **if** block and print output "**Congrats!, You are eligible to get hostel seat**". On failure the control enters into the body of else block and prints output "**Sorry!Better luck next time**".

5. Priya and Yashi are best friends in a college, one day they had a discussion that who is taller among them, then they went to the college nursery to record their heights. Write a C program to find who is taller among them. Note:- both are not in same size.

Program:-

```
#include <stdio.h>
int main()
{
float p_height, y_height;
printf("Enter height of Priya_:");
scanf("%f \n", &p_height);
printf("Enter height of Yashi_:");
scanf("%f\n", &y_height);
if(p_height>y_height)
{
printf("Priya is taller than Yashi");
}
else
{
printf("Priya is shorter than Yashi");
}
}
```

Output: -

Enter height of Priya_:6
Enter height of Yashi_:5.8
Priya is taller than Yashi
Enter height of Priya_:5.7
Enter height of Yashi_:5.9
Priya is shorter than Yashi

Explanation:-

In the above program

1. Declare a variables **p_height, y_height.**
2. Read the data from the keyboard using scanf() and stored in **p_ height and y_height.**

3. Check the condition, i.e. **if (p_height>y_height)**, On success the control enters into the body of **if** block and print output **"Priya is taller than Yashi"**. On failure, the control enters into the body of the **else** block and print output **"Priya is shorter than Yashi "**.

6. In a town there is a private bank with a huge crowd, due to this the bankmanager come up with a rule, depositors are allowed only on odd days in a month. Write a C program for above problem.

Program:-

```
#include <stdio.h>
int main()
{
int day;
printf("Enter day no._:");
scanf("%d", &day);
if(day%2==0 && day<32)
{
printf("Depositors are not allowed");
}
else
{
printf("Depositors are allowed");
}
return 0;
}
```

Output: -

```
Enter day no._:26
Depositors are not allowed
Enter day no._:19
Depositors are allowed
```

Explanation: -

In above program

1. Declare a variable **'day'**.

2. Read the data from the keyboard using **scanf()** and the data stored in a variable **'day'**.
3. Check the condition, i.e. **if (day%2!=0)**, on success the control enters into the body of the **if** block and print output **"depositors are allowed"**. On failure the control enters into the body of the **else** block and print output **"Depositors are not allowed"**.

Case Study of 'if' Clause

Case-1:- if(0):-

```
int main()
{
if(0)
{
printf("true");
}
else
{
printf("false");
}
return 0;
}
```

Note:- if (non-zero), it returns true,
if (zero), it returns false

Explanation:-

In the above program, Check the condition, i.e. **if (0)**, On success it enters into the body of the **if** block and prints **"true"**, On failure it prints **"false"**.

Case-2:- if(24):-

```
main()
{
if(24)
{
printf("true");
}
else
{
```

```
printf("false");
}
return 0;
}
```

Explanation:-

In the above program, check the condition, i.e. **if(24)** here the condition is similar to **if (non zero)**, then **if** returns true. if (zero) it returns false here output is "**true**", because it is non zero.

Case-3:- if (1, 0):-

```
main()
{
if(1, 0)
{
printf("true");
}
else
{
printf("false");
}
}
```

Output:-false

Explanation:-

In the above program, the output is "false " because when multiple values are separated with comma operator within the braces, then values which is right most to the comma considered as the result of the expression. In condition **if (1, 0),** the value right most of the comma is **zero**, then **if** condition returns false and control enters into the body of the else.

Multi way Selection :

if...else...if Ladder

If a user can have more than two options, based on logical condition it selects one among them. In this type of situation better to go with if-else-if ladder.If-else-if ladder executes from top to bottom. If first logical control is true, then the control goes to body of that block, otherwise the control goes to another logical condition and so on.

In case, if above all the logical conditions are false, then by default else block executes.

Syntax:

```
if(condition1)
{
//statements 1;
}
else if(condition2)
{
//statements 2;
}
else if(condition3)
{
//statement 3;
else
{
//statements 4;
}
```

Explanation:

1. Check the condition, i.e. **if (condition1)**.On success, it executes "**statements 1**"and ignores remaining logical conditions. On failure, it goes to step2.
2. Again check the condition, i.e. **else if (condition2)**. On success, it executes "**statements 2**" and ignores remaining logical conditions. On failure, it goes to step 3.
3. Finally check the condition, i.e. **else if (condition3)**. On success, it executes "**statements 3**". On failure, the control goes to **else** condition and executes "**statements 4**".

Flowchart :

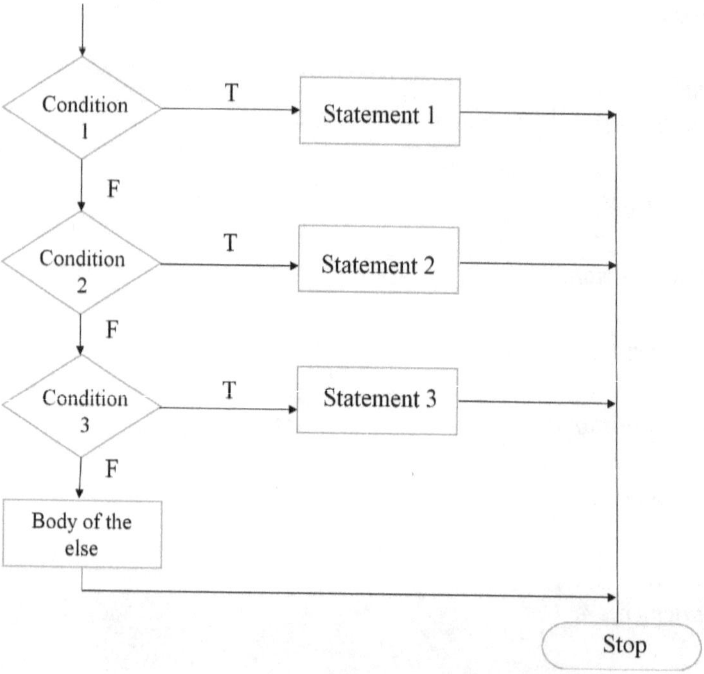

Figure 2.3 Flow Chart for If-Else Ladder

Example programs:

1. A University vice chancellor needs a software (program) in which, a student enters his four semesters percentage, then the software should calculate overall percentage of a particular student andthen based on that percentage prints the output.

Percentage	Result
>90	Distinction with 1st class
>80 and <90	1 st class
>70 and <80	2 nd class
>60 and <70	3 rd class
>50 and <60	With held
<=50	Not promoted

Program:

```
#include <stdio.h>
int main()
{
float sem1, sem2, sem3, sem4, per;
printf("Enter semester 1 percentage:");
scanf("%f", &sem1);
printf("Enter semester 2 percentage:");
scanf("%f", &sem2);
printf("Enter semester 3 percentage:");
scanf("%f", &sem3);
printf("Enter semester 4 percentage:");
scanf("%f", &sem4);
per=(sem1+sem2+sem3+sem4)/4;
if(per>90)
{
printf("Distinction with first class");
}
else if(per>80 && per<=90)
{
printf(" First class");
}
else if(per>70 && per<=80)
```

```
{
printf(" Second class");
}
else if(per>60 && per<=70){
printf(" Third class");
}
else if(per>50 && per<=60){
printf("With held");
}
else{
printf("Not promoted");
}
}
```

Output:

Enter semester 1 percentage:70
Enter semester 2 percentage:85
Enter semester 3 percentage:83
Enter semester 4 percentage:86
First class
Enter semester 1 percentage:35
Enter semester 2 percentage:25
Enter semester 3 percentage:36
Enter semester 4 percentage:21
Not promoted

Explanation:

In the above program

1. Declare variables **sem1, sem2, sem3 and sem4** percentage.
2. Read the **sem1, sem2, sem3 and sem4** percentagevalues from keyboard using**scanf** ().
3. Calculate average percentage of all four semesters and store the value invariable "**per**".
4. Check the condition, i.e. **if (per>90)**.On success, the control enters into the body of the **if** block and prints output "**Distinction with first class**". On failure, the control goes to next condition, i.e. **else if (per>80 && per<=90).**

2. Mr. Kiran conducted a game for a prize money. The game rule is the box contains 3 chits and the player has to pick one among them and the prize money is? If

Condition	Print statement
Number>0	Rs 24, 000/-
Number=0	Rs 50, 000/-
Number<0	Sorry! Try again

Program:

```
#include <stdio.h>
int main()
{
int number;
printf("Enter any number:");
scanf("%d", &number);
if(number>0)
{
printf("You win Rs 24, 000/-");
}
else if(number==0)
{
printf("You win Rs 50, 000/-");
}
 else
{
printf("Sorry! try again");
}
return 0;
}
```

Output:

Enter any number:2
You win Rs 24, 000/-
Enter any number:-3

Sorry! try again

Explanation:

In the above program

1. Read the **number**.
2. Check the condition, i.e. **if (number>0)**. On success, it prints "**You win Rs 24, 000 /-**". Onfailure, it goes to step 3.
3. Check the condition, i.e. else **if (number==0).** On success, it prints "**Youwin Rs 50, 000** /-".On failure, it goes to step 4.
4. If above all the conditions fails, then by default, **else** executes and prints "**Sorry! Try again**".

3. Ask the user to enter 3 different values and find biggest among them.

Program:

```
#include <stdio.h>
int main()
{
int d, p, k;
printf("Enter three values:");
scanf("%d %d %d", &d, &p, &k);
if(d>p &&d<k )
{
printf("%d is big", d);
}
else if(p>d &&p>k )
{
printf("%d is big", p);
}
else
{
printf("%d is big", k);
}
return 0;
}
```

Output:

Enter three values : 5 6 7

7 is big

Explanation:

In the above program

1. Read 3 values.
2. Check the condition, i.e. **if (d>p && d>k).** On success, prints **"d value is big"**. On failure, go to step3.
3. Check the condition, i.e. else **if (p>d && p>k)**. On success, prints **"p value is big"**.On failure, go to step4.
4. Above all the conditions are false, then by default **else** executes and prints **"k value is big"**.

4. Ask user to enter a positive value, in between 1 to 4 then print the relevant roman number. If value>4 then print "Sorry! Wrong entry".

Program:

```
#include <stdio.h>
int main()
{
int k;
printf("Enter the value between 1 to 4: ");
scanf("%d", &k);
if(k==1)
{
printf("Roman value for 1 is I");
}
else if(k==2)
{
printf("Roman value for 2 is II");
}
else if(k==3)
{
printf("Roman value for 3 is III");
}
else if(k==4)
{
printf("Roman value for 4 is IV");
}
else
```

```
{
printf("Sorry! Wrong entry");
}
return 0;
}
```

Output:

Enterthe value between 1 to 4: 4

Roman value for 4 is IV

Explanation:

In the above program:

1. Read the number.
2. Check the condition, i.e. **if (k==1).** On success, prints "**Roman value of 1 is I**". On failure, it goes to step 3.
3. Check the condition, i.e. **if (k==2).** On success, prints "**Roman value of 2 is II** ". On failure, it goes to step 4.
4. Check the condition, i.e. **if (k==3).** On success, prints "**Roman value of 3 is III** ". On failure, it goes to step 5.
5. Check the condition, i.e. **if (k==4).** On success, prints "**Roman value of 4 is IV** ". On failure, it goes to step 6.
6. If above all the conditionsfails by default, **else** executes and prints "**Sorry! Wrong entry**".

5. Ask the user to enter the 3 integer values of the triangle, if

Condition	Print statement
All sides are equal	Print equilateral triangle
Any two sides are equal	Isosceles triangle
None of the sides are equal	Scalene triangle

Program:

```
#include <stdio.h>
int main()
{
int s1, s2, s3;
printf("Enter 3 sides of a triangle:");
scanf("%d %d %d ", &s1, &s2, &s3);
if(s1==s2 && s2==s3 && s1==s3)
{
printf("Equilateral triangle");
}
else if(s1==s2||s2==s3||s3==s1)
{
printf("Isosceles triangle");
}
else
{
printf("Scalene triangle");
}
return 0;
}
```

Output:

Enter 3 sides of a triangle:4 3 4
Isosceles triangle

Explanation:

In the above program:

1. Read the three sides of a triangle.
2. Check the condition, i.e. **if (s1==s2==s3)**, On success, it prints **"Equilateral triangle"**. On failure, goes to step 3.
3. Check the condition, i.e. **else if (s1==s2||s2==s3||s3==s1).** On success, it prints **"Isosceles triangle"**. On failure, goes to step 4.
4. If above all the conditions are failed then by default **else** executes and prints **"Scalene triangle"**.

Nested if Statement

Wrapping up of one or more if-else statements in the body of another '**if**' or '**else**' statement is called **nested if.**

Syntax:

```
if(condition 1)
{
if(condition 2)
{
//statements//;
}
}
else
{
if(condition 3)
{
//statements//;
}
}
```

Explanation:

In the above syntax

1. Check condition, i.e. **if (condition 1)**, On success, go to step 2. On failure, go to step 3.
2. Check condition, i.e. **if (condition 2)**, On success, go to **if** block and execute statements. On failure, control goes out from **if (condition 2)** block.
3. On failure of **condition 1**, control goes to **else** block and check condition i.e. if**(condition 3)**, On success, goes to **if** block and executes statements. On failure, control goes out from the block.

Flowchart :

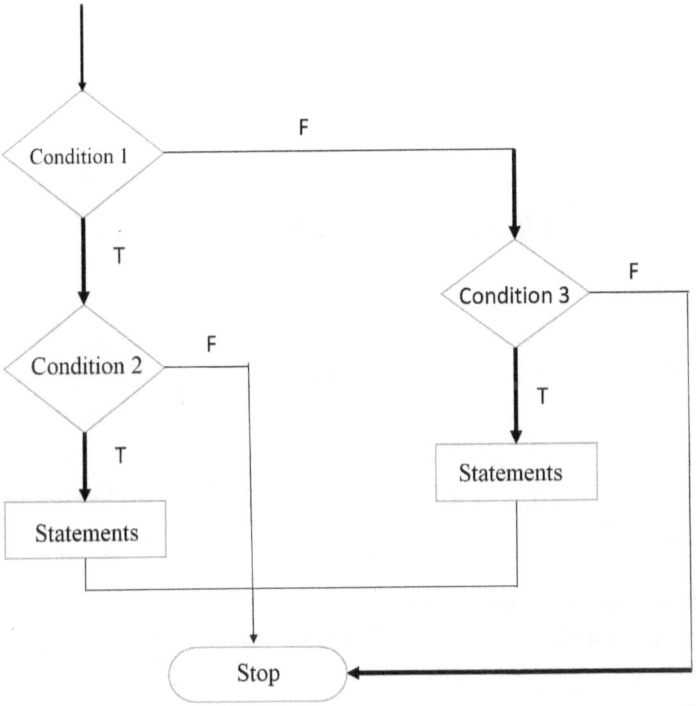

Figure 2.4 Flow Chart for Nested if

Example Programs: -

1. The government announces age limit to apply for government jobs

- The age of candidate is not less than 18.
- The age of the candidate is not greater than 32.

Program:

```
#include <stdio.h>
void main()
{
int cand_age;
printf("Enter the age of the candidate:");
```

```
scanf("%d", &cand_age);
if(cand_age<18)
{
printf("Sorry! Age of the candidate is not less than 18");
}
else
{
if(cand_age<32)
{
printf("Congrats! Eligible to get government job");
}
else
{
printf("Sorry! you are too old and not eligible");
}
}
}
```

Output:

```
Enter the age of the candidate:24
Congrats! Eligible to get government job
```

Explanation:

In the above program

1. Read the candidate age.
2. Check condition, i.e. **if (cand_age<18)**. On success, it prints "**Sorry!, Age of the candidate is not less than 18**". On failure, goes to **else** block.
3. Control enters into else block and checks condition, i.e. **if(cand_age<32)**. On success, it prints "**Congrats! Eligible to get government job**". On failure, it prints "**Sorry! You are too old and not eligible**".

2. The deemed university conducts an eligibility test to give seat in that university and based on that rank, the system automatically allocates the department in that university.

- if rank=>1 and rank<=10, Eligible to get seat and otherwise no seat.

- if rank>=1 and rank<=5, Eligible to get seat in computer department.
- if rank>=6 and rank<=10, Eligible to get a seat in core branch.

Program:

```
#include <stdio.h>
void main()
{
int rank;
printf("Enter rank of eligibility test:");
scanf("%d", &rank);
if(rank>=1 && rank<=10)
{
if(rank>=1 && rank<=5)
{
printf("Eligible to get seat in computer department");
}
else
{
printf("Eligible to get a seat in core branch");
}
}
else
{
printf("Rank is too high, you are not eligible");
}
}
```

Output:

Enter rank of eligibility test:7
Eligible to get a seat in core branch
Enter rank of eligibility test:15
Rank is too high, you are not eligible

Explanation:

In the above program

1. Read the rank got on eligibility test.

2. Check condition, i.e. **if (rank=>1 && rank<=10)**.On success, control goes to step3. On failure, control goes to **else** block and prints "**Rank is too high, you are not eligible**".
3. Check condition i.e. **if(rank>=1 && rank<=5)**. On success, it prints "**Eligible to get seat in computer department**". On failure, it prints "**Eligible to get a seat in core branch**".

Switch Statement:

The switch statement is similar to the if - else ladder. When comparing to if-else ladder is very easy to understand and easy to read.

Working:

The value of an expression / variable in switch statement composes with case value. In case expression/variable value and case value is same, then the control stops there and executes block of statements belongs to that particular case.

In case expression /variable value and case value is not same, then control goes to default statement and executes block of statements belongs to default statement and control goes out from switch statement.

Syntax:

```
switch(expression)
{
case value1: //statements;
break;
case value2: //statements;
break;
case valuen: //statements;
break;
default: //statements;
```

Explanation:

In above syntax

1. Expression value is matched with any of the case value, then executes the statements belongs to that particular case and after break

statement evaluates the control comes out from the switch statement.

2. In case no match founds then, default statement executes.

Basic Rules for switch Statement:

1. **switch Expression or Variable:**The type of an expression/variable must be integer or character.
2. **case Value:**The type of case value must be an integer or character. Case value must present inner to the switch statement.
3. **break Statement:**The break statement is not mandatory in switch statement.In case break statement evaluates, then the control comes out from the switch statement.

Flowchart:

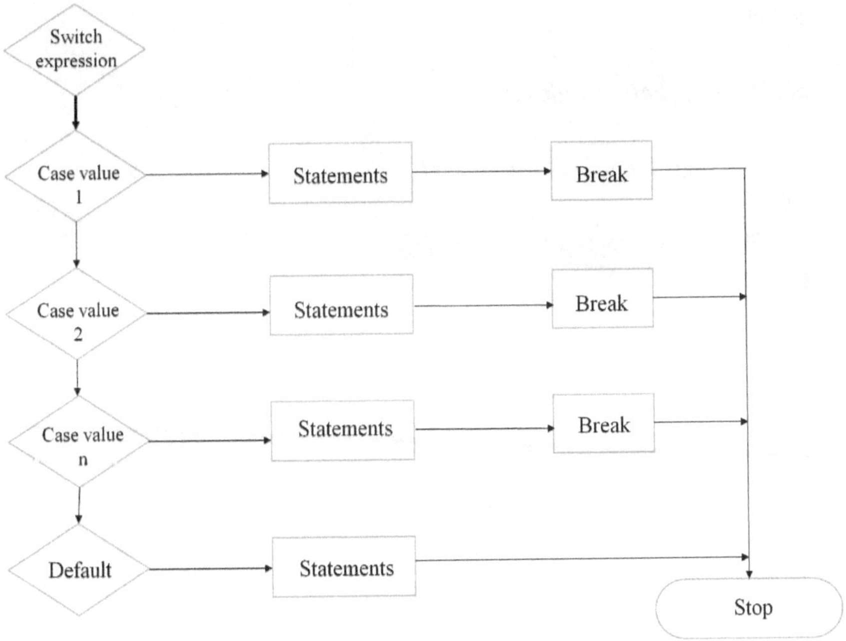

Figure 2.5 Flowchart of switch

Example Programs :

1. Ask user to enter a positive value denoting k and follow the rules

- **If the number is 1>=k<=4, then print roman number corresponding to the number.**
- **if number is k>4, print "Sorry! Wrong entry".**

Write a C program using a switch statement.

Program:

```
#include <stdio.h>
void main()
[
int k;
printf("Enter k value:");
scanf("%d", &k);
switch(k)
[
case 1:printf("Roman value for 1 is I");
break;
case 2:printf("Roman value for 2 is II");
break;
case 3:printf("Roman value for 3 is III");
break;
case 4:printf("Roman value for 4 is IV");
break;
default: printf("Sorry!Wrong entry");
]
]
```

Output:

Enter k value:2

Roman value for 2 is II

Explanation:

In the above program

1. Read the **k** value.

2. Check condition i.e., **switch (k)**, the expression/variable value matches with any of the case values then executes the relevant case block.
3. The expression or variable doesn't match with any case value, then executes default statements and prints "**Sorry! Wrong entry**".

2. In a town there is a private bank with a huge crowd, due to this the bank manager came up with a new rule, deposits are allowed only on odd days of the month. Write a C program for above problem using a switch statement.

Program: -

```
#include <stdio.h>
int main()
{
int day;
printf("Enter day no:");
scanf("%d", &day);
if(day<32)
{
switch(day%2)
{
case 0: printf("Deposits are not allowed");
break;
case 1: printf("Deposits are allowed");
break;
}
}
return 0;
}
```

Output:

```
Enter day no : 4
Deposits are not allowed

Enter day no:21
Deposits are allowed
```

Explanation:

In the above program

1. Read the day value.

2. Check the condition, i.e. **if (day<32)**. If the condition is true, then checks the condition, i.e. **switch (day%2)**, the expression value matches with any of the case values then, executes the relevant case block.

3. A shopping mall conducts a festival sale with discount on the amount. If the purchase amount is greater than 5000 rupees, give 20% discount. Write a c program to calculate the net amount after discount using switch statement.

Program:

```
#include<stdio.h>
int main()
{
double amount, discount, sale_price;
printf("Enter the purchased amount:");
scanf("%lf", &amount);
switch(amount>5000)
{
case 0:discount=(amount*5)/100;
sale_price=amount-discount;
printf("Net amount after discount is:%lf", sale_price);
break;
case 1:discount=(amount*20)/100;
sale_price=amount-discount;
printf("Net amount after discount is:%lf", sale_price);
break;
}
return 0;
}
```

Output:

Enter the purchased amount:3700
Net amount after discount is:3515.000000

Explanation:

In the above program

1. Read purchase amount.
2. Check the condition, i.e. **switch (amount>5000)** if it returns 0 or 1 based on amount. The expression or variable matches with any case value the executes the relevant case block.

4. Request a user to enter a letter from (A to Z) /(a to z). If any letter is vowel, then, based on the following table print the result.

Letter	Print
A, I, O	This is top 7 most used letter in English and it is vowel.
E	Most common letter in English and it is vowel.
U	It is vowel and common letter.
Apart from A, E, I, O, U	It is consonant.

Program:

```
#include <stdio.h>
int main()
{
char letter;
printf("Enter any letter from a to z:");
scanf("%c", &letter);
switch(letter)
{
case ‘A’:
case ‘a’:
case ‘I’:
case ‘i’:
case ‘O’:
```

```
case 'o':printf("This is top 7 most used letter in English and it is vowel");
break;
case 'E':
case 'e':printf("This is top used letter in English and it is vowel");
break;
case 'U':
case 'u':printf("It is vowel and common letter");
break;
default: printf("It is consonant");
}
return 0;
}
```

Output:

Enter any letter from a to z:U
It is vowel and common letter

Explanation:

In the above program

1. Read the letter from **(A to Z) /(a to z).**
2. Check the condition, i.e. **switch (letter),** the expression/variable matches with the corresponding case, then, the relevant case statement will be executed.
3. The expression/variable doesn't match with the case value, then, default statement will be executed.

5. A university designs a software to know the grade and mark range by giving grade point as an input. The following table is used.

Grade point	Mark range	Grades
10	91-100	A
9	81-90	B
8	70-80	C
7	60-71	D
6	<60	F

Program:

```
#include <stdio.h>
int main() {
int points;
printf("Enter grade point:");
scanf("%d", &points);
switch(points)
{
case 6:printf("Grade: F, marks range:<60");
break;
case 7:printf("Grade: D, marks range:60-71");
break;
case 8:printf("Grade: C, marks range:70-80");
break;
case 9:printf("Grade: B, marks range:81-90");
break;
case 10:printf("Grade: A, marks range:91-100");
break;
default: printf("Wrong entry");
}
```

Output:

Enter grade point:8

Grade: C, marks range:70-80

Explanation:

In the above program

1. Readpoints.
2. Checks the condition, i.e. **switch (points).**
3. If points=**6**, then prints "**Grade: F, marks, ranges: <60**".
4. If points=**7**, then prints "**Grade: D, marks, ranges: 60-71**".
5. If points=**8**, then prints "**Grade: C, marks, ranges: 70-80**".
6. If points=**9**, then prints "**Grade: B, marks range: 81-90**".
7. If points=**10**, then prints "**Grade: A, marks range: 91-100**".
8. If the points don't match with the case value, thendefault statement executes and prints "**Wrong entry**"

Case Study On Switch Statement

Case 1:With break statement in switch

Whenever the break statement evaluates then the control comes out of the block (comes out from the switch statement), due to this the control doesn't check the following case values.

Program:

```
#include <stdio.h>
int main(){
int k=1;
switch(k)
{
case 1:printf("one");
break;
case 2:printf("two");
break;
case 3:printf("three");
break;
default: printf("wrong entry");
}
return 0;
}
```

Output: one

Explanation:

In the above program

1. Read the k value.
2. Check condition i.e. **switch(k)**, here k=1 the value matches with case 1 and prints "**one**" then evaluates the break statement and then comes out from the switch statement.

Case 2: Without break in Switch Statement

If there is no break statement in switch case, all the cases will execute after the matching case.

Program:

```
#include <stdio.h>
int main()
{
int k=2;
switch(k)
{
case 1:printf("one\n");
case 2:printf("two\n");
case 3:printf("three\n");
default: printf("wrong entry");
}
return 0;
}
}
```

Output:

```
two
three
wrong entry
```

Explanation:

In the above program

1. Here k=2.
2. Check condition **switch(k).**
3. The variable **k** matches with **case 2** and prints **'two'** and next time there is no break statement after case 2. Remaining case values also executes, including a default statement. since, there is no break statement in between case values.

Case 3: Put default block in any place

In switch statement, there is no rule for placing the default block. This can be anywhere in the switch statement.

Firstly, control checks for the case values if it is matched, it ignores remaining case values. In casecase values are not matched, then control checks for default statement.

Program:

```
#include <stdio.h>
int main() {
int k=24;
switch(k)
{
default: printf("Wrong entry");
break;
case 1:printf("one");
break;
case 2:printf("two");
break;
case 3:printf("three");
}
return 0;
}
```

Output: Wrong entry

Explanation:

In the above program

1. Read k value.
2. Check the condition **switch(k).**
3. Control checks **k=24** with all the case values up to case 3 then, no match found, then control checks for default statements and executes the default statements and prints **"Wrong entry"**.

4. STANDARD FUNCTIONS :

These are built In functions. The built-in functions are resides in header file.

The standard functions are also called as pre-defined functions or library functions.

For instance printf( ),scanf( ),getch( ) are defined in header file stdio.h.

In C programming we have the following header files

1. stdio.h :

It is used to include information for input Or output-related functions.

It makes coding easier@ because no need to write code for input and output functions.

Example program to illustrate <stdio h> header file.

```
#include<stdio.h>
main( )
{
int a,b,c;
printf("Enter a,b values");
printf("%d %d ",&a,&b);
printf("Sum is %d ",a+b);
}
```

2. math.h :

It is used to include information for mathematical operations like sqrt( ),abs( ),floor( )and pow( ) etc..

Example program to illustrate <math.h> header file.

```
#include<stdio.h>
#include<math.h>
Void main( )
{
int a =10, b = 20;
printf("%d",sqrt(a));
printf("%d",pow(a,2));
printf("%d",floor(24.29));
}
```

3. string.h :

It is used to include information for string handling functions like strlen(),strcpy(),strcmp( ),and strcat( ) etc..

Example program to illustrate <string.h> header file.

```
#include<stdio.h>
#include<string.h>
```

```
main( )
{
Char a[100] = "Manasa",b[100] ="Koti";
printf("%d",strlen(a));
printf("%d",strcat(b,a));
printf("%d",strcmp(a,b));
}
```

4.stdlib.h :

It is used to include information for general functions like malloc( ), calloc( ), free( ), realloc( ), atoi( ),atoll( ) and rand( ).

5.float.h :

It is used to in lude information for FLT_MIN,FLT_MAX,DBL_MIN and DBL_MAX.

Example program to illustrate <float.h> header file.

```
#inlcude<stdio.h>
#inlcude<float.h>
main( )
{
printf("MAX VALUE for float = %d \n",FLT_MAX);
printf("MIN VALUE for float = %d \n",FLT_MIN);
printf("MAX VALUE for double = %d \n",DBL_MAX);
printf("MIN VALUE for double = %d \n",DBL_MAX);
}
```

5. REPITITION :

Concept of Loops :

Repeating same block of code again and again until the condition is false.

C programming comes up with 3 types of loops:

Pre-Test Loops :

- for loop
- while loop

Post-Test Loops :

- do - while loop

Pre-Test Loops :

for Loop:

For loop is easy, important and regularly used in arrays and linked lists etc.

Syntax:

for (**initialization** ; **condition** ; **update_statements**)
{
//Body of the for loop
}

Explanation:

In the above syntax

1. Initially, Control executes **initialization** step and this step executes only once at beginning of the loop.
2. Next control goes to **condition** step.

    - If the condition is true, then control goes to step 3.
    - If the condition is false, then the for loop will ends.

3. If condition is true in step 2, then the control executes**statements** present in for loop.
4. After step 3, the control goes to **update statements**.Update statement means increment or decrement the counter variable.
5. After step 4, the control again goes to condition step (Step 2) and if the condition is true, repeats the step 3, step 4 and step 5 until the condition is false.

Flow Chart:

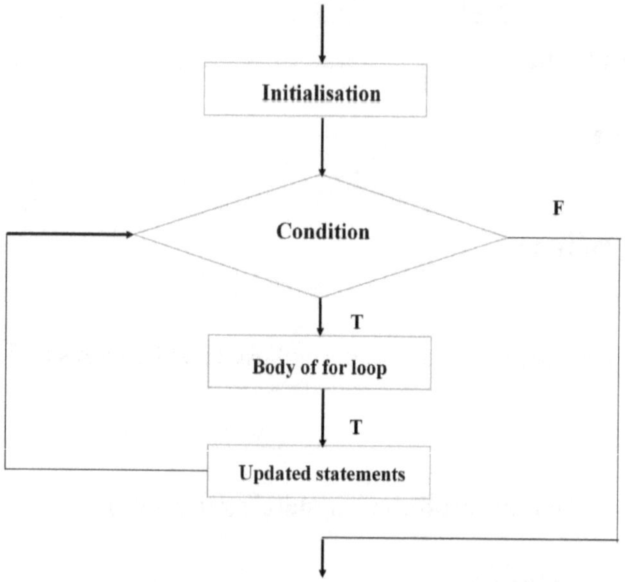

Figure 2.6 Flow Chart for *for* Loop

Example Programs:

1. Design a C program to print first n natural number(s) using for loop?

Program:

```
#include<stdio.h>
voidmain()
{
int k;
printf ("Enter value "); scanf ("%d", &k );
for ( int p=1; p<=k; p++)
{
printf("%d\t", p);
}
}
```

Output:

```
Enter value 4
1 2 3 4
```

Explanation:

In the above program

1. Read **k** value.
2. Set **p=1.**
3. Check condition, i.e. **(p<=k)** (k value is 4), the condition looks **1<=4**, as 1 is less than or equal to 4 is true and prints **1** (**values of p**).
4. After that the control excutes next update statement and then P valuebecomes 2.
5. And again check the condition, i.e. **(p<=k).** Now above condition looks **2<=4**, as2 is less than or equal to 4 is true and prints **2** (**values of P**).
6. Above process repeats until the condition becomes **5<=4**, because 5 is less than or equals to 4 is false and for loop ends.

2. Design a C program to read a positive value denoting K from the user and print Kto 1 using for loop.

Program:

```
#include<stdio.h>
void main()
{
int k;
printf ("Enter k value ");
scanf ("%d", &k );
for ( int p=k; p>=1; p--)
{
printf("%d\t", p);
}
}
```

Output:

Enter k value 4
4 3 2 1

Explanation :

In the above program

1. Read **k** value.

2. Initialize **P** with value in k, **P=k** (k is 4).
3. Check condition, i.e. (**p>=1**) the condition looks **4>=1**, as 4 is greater than or equals to 1 is true and prints **4** (values of p).
4. And next update statement executesand P valuebecomes 3.
5. And again condition, i.e. (**p>=1**) executes, Now above condition looks **3>=1**, as2 is greater than or equals to 1 is true and prints **3** (**valuesofP**).
6. Above process repeats until the condition becomes **0>=1**, as 0 is greater than or equals to 1 is false and for loop ends.

3. Design a C program to read a positive value denoting K from the user and print even numbers in between firstk natural numbers using for loop.

Program:

```
#include<stdio.h>
void main()
{
int k, p;
printf("Enter k value ");
scanf("%d", &k); for(p=1;p<=k;p++)
{
if(p%2==0)
{
printf("%d iseven\n", p);
}
}
}
```

Output:

Enter k value 10 2 is even

4 is even

6 is even

8 is even

10 is even

Explanation:

In the above program

1. Read **k** value.
2. Initialize **p** with **1**.

3. Check condition, i.e. (**p<=k**) the condition looks **1<=10,** as 1 is less than or equals to 10 is true and executes condition **if (P%2==0)** i.e. (**1%2==0**), the condition is false and it does not print anything.
4. And next update statementexecutes and P value becomes 2.
5. And again condition, i.e. **(p<=k)** executes. Now above condition looks **2<=10** as 2 is less than or equals to 10 is true and executes condition **if (P%2==0)** i.e. **(2%2==0)** the condition is true and prints "**2 is even**".
6. Above process repeats until the condition becomes **11<=10**, as 11 is less than or equals to 10 is false and for loop ends.

4. Design a C program to read a positive value from the user and print multiplication table of that number.

Program:

```
#include<stdio.h>
void main()
{
int table, k;
printf("Enter multiplication table number ");
scanf("%d*%d=%d\n", &table);
for(k=1;k<=5;k++)
{
printf ("%d*%d=%d \n", k, table, k*table);
}
}
```

Output:

Enter multiplication table number 2 1*2=2
2*2=4
3*2=6
4*2=8
5*2=10

Explanation:

In the above program

1. Read multiplication table number.
2. Initialize k with 1.

3. Check condition, i.e. **k <=5** the condition looks **1<=5,** as 1 is less than or equal to 5 is true, the control goes to for loop bodyand prints **"1*2=2"**.
4. And next update statement executes and k value becomes 2.
5. And againexcutes the condition, i.e. **(k<=5)**. Now condition looks like**2<=5,** as2 is less than or equalsto 5 is true, then control goes to for loop body and prints **"2*2=4"**.
6. Above process repeats until the condition becomes **6<=5,** as 6 is less than or equals to 5 is false and for loop ends.

5. Design a C program to read a positive value and print factorial of a given number.

Program:

```
#include<stdio.h>
void main()
{
intfact_no=1, p, value; printf("Enter number ");
scanf("%d", &value); for(p=1; p<=value; p++)
{
fact_no=fact_no*p;
}
printf("Factorial of %d: %d", value, fact_no);
}
```

Output:

Enter number 4
Factorial of 4: 24

Explanation:

In the above program

1. Read a **value** to find factorial.
2. Initialize fact_**no=1, p=1.**
3. Check condition, i.e. **(P<=value**) the condition looks **1<=4,** it is true, then control goes to **for loop** body and evaluate **fact_no=fact_no*p (fact_no=1*1).**
4. Update statement executes and P value becomes 2.
5. And again condition, i.e. (**p<=value**), the condition looks like **2<=4,** it is true, then controlled goes to for loop body and evaluate

fact_no=fact_no*P (fact_no=1*2).

6. Above process repeats until the condition becomes **5<=4**, it is false and for loop ends.

Case Study on for Loop

Case-1: The result of semicolon next to "for" loop Program:

```
#include<stdio.h>
    void main()
    {
    int p; for(p=1;p<=4;p++);
    {
    printf("C programming");
    }
    }
```

Output:

C programming

Explanation:

In the above program

1. Variable p value set to 1.
2. Condition **p<=4** means this for loop iterates 4 times but the control does not enter into **for** body, because the semicolon after the for loop indicates that there is no body for this for loop, due to this the control does not goes into for loop body.
3. Whenever the condition becomes false, i.e. **(5<=4)** then print statement executes and print "**C programming**"

Note:

Whenever there is a semicolon next to for loop, the compiler thinks that there is a for loop without body.

Case-2: Without Initialization and Update Statements Program:

```
#include<stdio.h>
main()
```

```
{
int p=1;
for( ;p<=4; )
{
printf("%d\t", p); p++;
}
}
```

Output:

1 2 3 4

Explanation:

In the above program

The for loop iterates 4 times and prints 1 2 3 4 as output

Note:

In for loop initialization, condition and update statement is optional, but the semicolon is mandatory in between statements.

Case3: With multiple initialization, condition and update statements

Program:

```
#include<stdio.h>
void main()
{
int p, k;
for(p=1, k=1; p>=6, k<=5; p++, k++)
{
printf("p=%d and k=%d\n", p, k);
}
}
```

In the above program

1. Comma operator has last priority.
2. Comma operator executes left to right.
3. When there is one or more conditions in for loop separated by comma's then the compiler executes all the conditions from left to right, but based on the utmost right condition (the termination and iteration will happen).

Output:

P=1 and k=1 P=2 and k=2

P=3 and k=3 P=4 and k=4 P=5 and k=5

Explanation:

In the above program

1. Initialize **p=1, k=1** (comma operates executes left to right).
2. Check condition (**p>=6, k<=5**) in the above for loop executes until the condition **k<=5** is false, because the compiler consider the utmost right condition (**k<=5**) to terminate the loop.

while Loop

Flowchart :

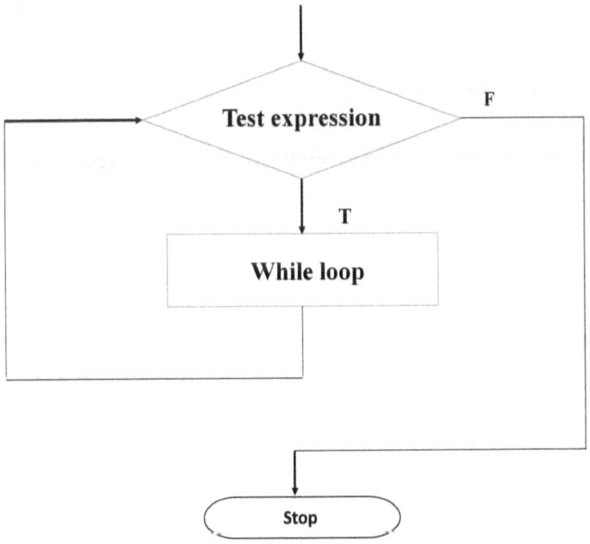

Figure 2.7 Flowchart of while loop

Loop iterates the block of statements until the condition is false.

- It is also called entry-controlled loop (or) pre-tested loop.
- In the while loop, the condition restricts the entry of the control into the body of the while.
- If the condition is true, control enters into the while loop body and executes the block of code repeatedly until condition fails.

Syntax:

```
while (condition)
{
//statements;
// update statements;
}
```

Explanation:

1. The control executes the condition.
2. The condition is true, the control executes and updates the statements present in the while loop body.
3. Again the control goes to step 1 and repeats until the condition fails.

Example Programs:

1. Design a C program to read a positive value 'k' from users and Print Natural numbers from 1 to k using while loop.

Program:

```
#include<stdio.h>
void main()
{
int p=1, k;
printf("Enter value ");
scanf("%d", &k);
while(p<=k)
{
printf("%d \t", p); p++;
}
}
```

Output:

Enter value 4
1 2 3 4

Explanation:

1. Read the value of 'k' and assign p=1.
2. Check the condition while (p<=k). If the condition is true, control enters the while loop and executes the print statement and updates p value. Again repeats this step.
3. If the condition is false, the control exits the loop.

2. Design a C program to read a positive value 'k' from the programmer and Print k to 1 using while loop.

Program:

```
#include<stdio.h>
void main()
[
int p=1, k; printf("Enter k value ");
scanf("%d", &k);
while(k>=p)
[
printf("%d \t", k); k--;
]
]
```

Output:

Enter k value 4
4 3 2 1

Explanation:

1. Read the value of 'k' and assign p=1.
2. Check the condition while (k>=p). If the condition is true, control enters the while loop and executes the print statement and updates p value. Again repeats this step.
3. If the condition is false, the control exits the loop.

3. Design a C program to read a positive integer 'k' from the user and Print sum of digits of the number (make use of the while loop).

Program:

```
#include<stdio.h>
void main()
{
int k, rem, sum=0;
printf("Enter the number ");
scanf("%d", &k);
while(k>0)
{
rem=k%10;
sum=sum+rem; k=k/10;
}
printf("Sum of the digits ofa given number is %d", sum);
}
```

Output:

Enter the number 2429
Sum of the digits of a given number is 17

Explanation:

1. Read the value of 'k'.
2. Check the condition while (k>0).
3. If the condition is true, control enters the while loop and executes the statements rem=k%10, sum=sum + rem, and k=k/10.
4. Again repeats the steps 2&3.
5. If the condition is false, the control exits the loop.

4. Design a C program to read a positive value 'k' from users and Print Even numbers from 1 to k (Use while loop).

Program:

```
#include<stdio.h>
void main()
{
```

```
int k, p=1;
printf("Enter k value ");
scanf("%d", &k);
while(p<=k)
{
if(p%2==0)
{
printf("%d \t", p);
}
p++;
}
}
```

Output:-

Enter k value 10
2 4 6 8 10

Explanation:

1. Read 'k' value and assign p=1.
2. Check the condition, i.e., while (p<=k).
3. If the condition is true, the control enters the while loop and checks the condition if (p%2==0). If this is true, it prints the even numbers and update its value.
4. Until the condition (p<=k) fails, steps 2 and 3 will be repeated.

Post-Test Loops :

do-while Loop:

- do-- while loop is of same nature as while, but with a small difference.
- In while loop testing condition is at the beginning of the loop, but in do-while the code is executed at least once and then the condition is checked.
- The body of do-while loop executes no less than one time, i.e., executed at least once.

Flowchart:

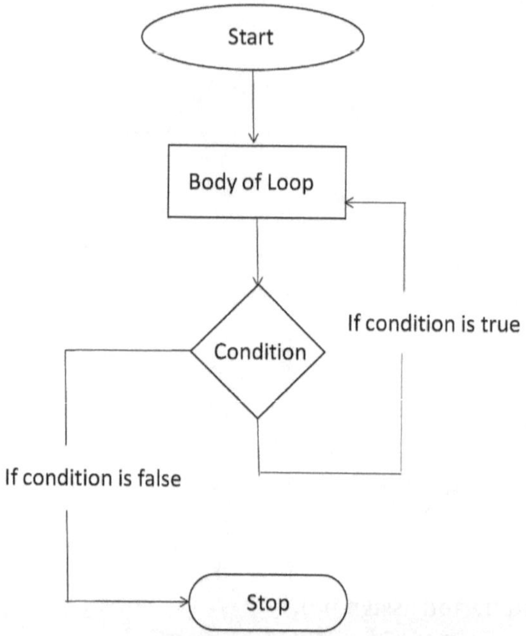

Figure 2.8 Flowchart of do-while

Syntax:

```
do
{
//statements;
//update statements;
} while(condition);
```

Explanation:

1. At first, the control executes statements in the body of **do.**
2. After step1, the test condition is executed.
3. If the test condition is true, then the control goes to step 1 until the condition fails.

Example programs:

1. Design a C program to read a positive value 'k' from the user and print 1 to k natural numbers using do- while loop.

Program:

```
#include<stdio.h>
void main()
{
int k, p=0;
printf("Enter k value");
scanf("%d", &k);
do
{
p++;
printf("%d \t", p);
}
while(p<k);
}
```

Output:

```
Enter k value5
1 2 3 4 5
```

Explanation:

1. Read k value and assign p=1.
2. The control executes the statements in the do-while body.
3. Next the control checks the condition (p<k).
4. If the above condition is true, the control goes to step2 and repeats until the condition is false.

2. Design a C program to read 3digit positive number 'k' from the user and check if it is an Armstrong number or not.

Program:

```
#include<stdio.h>
void main()
```

```
{
int k, temp, rem_val, result=0;
printf("Enter 3 digit number");
scanf("%d", &k);
temp=k;
do
{
rem_val=k%10;
result=result+( rem_val*rem_val*rem_val);
k=k/10;
}while(k>0);
if(temp==result)
{
printf("The given number %d isan Armstrong number", temp);
}
else
{
printf("The given number %d is not an Armstrong number", temp);
}
}
```

Output:

Enter 3 digit number253
The given number 253 is not an Armstrong number

Explanation:

1. Read the value of 'k', assign temp=k and result=0.
2. The control executes the statements rem_val=k%10, result=result+ (rem_val* rem_val* rem_val) and k=k/10.
3. Now the control checks the condition (k>0).
4. If the above condition is true, again the control goes to step2 until the condition is false.

3. Design a C program to read a 3digit positive number 'k' and Print the given number in reverse order (Use do-while loop).

Program:

```
#include<stdio.h>
void main()
{
int k, rev_val, rem_val;
printf("Enter 3digit positive number "); scanf("%d", &k);
do
{
rem_val=k%10; rev_val=rev_val*10+rem_val;
k=k/10;
}
while(k!=0);
printf("The reverse of given number is %d", rev_val);
}
```

Output:

Enter 3digit positive number 243 The reverse of given number is 342

Explanation:

1. Read ‘k’ value and assign rev_val=0.
2. The control executes the statements rem_val=k%10, rev_val=rev_val*10 + rem_val and k=k/10 till the condition k! =0 fails.
3. Next the control executes the print statement and prints the reverse value.

6. INITIALISATION AND UPDATING :

> *"Initialization expression executes only once in a loop lifetime.*
> *The initialization expression job must be done before the first execution of the loop body."*

Jazmin

Initialization For Pre-test Loop :

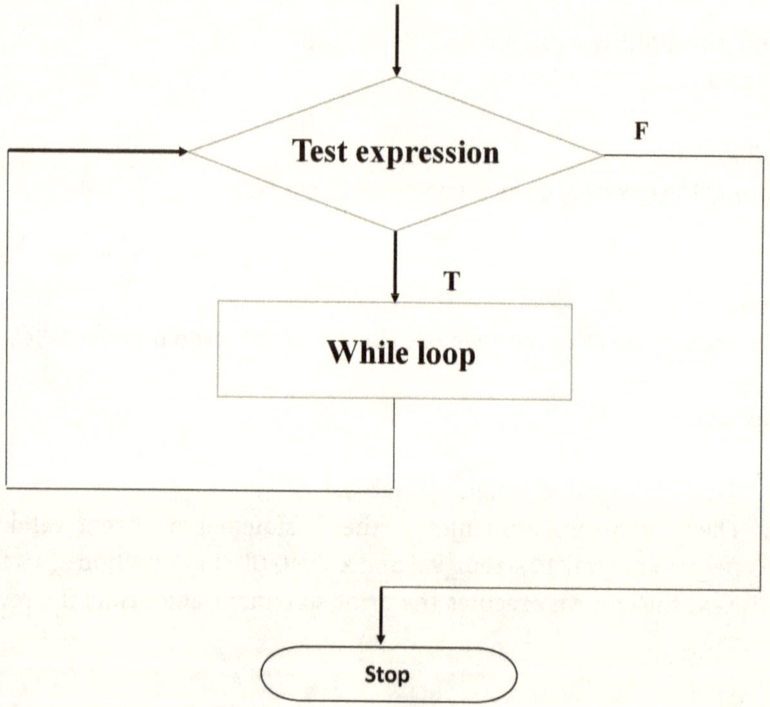

Figure 2.9 Flowchart of while loop

In the Pre-test loop, the initialization expression executes first and then checks the condition.

If the condition is true the loop will iterate until and unless the condition is false.

Here the king point is initialization expert executes only once.

Initialization For Post-test Loop :

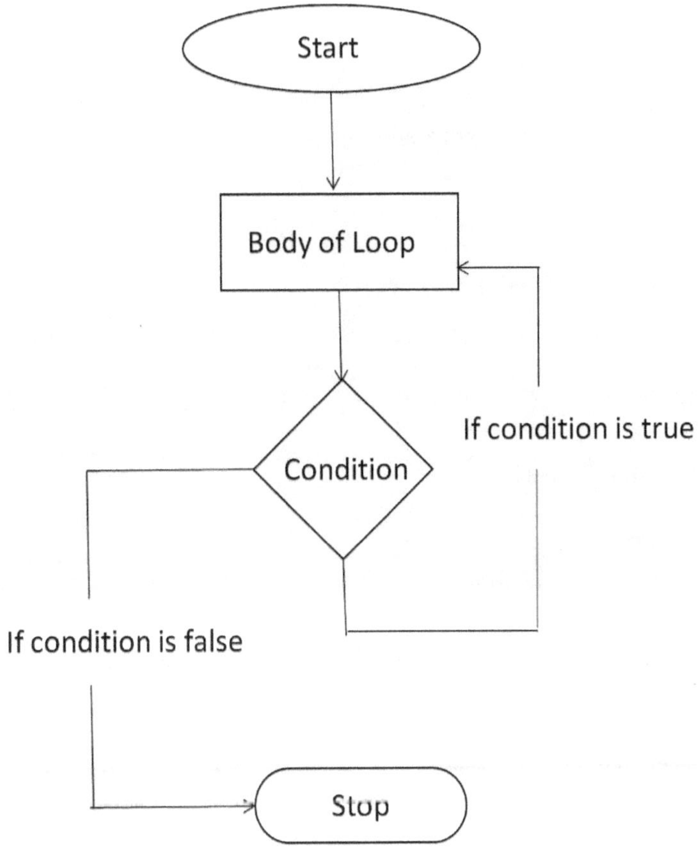

Figure 2.10 Flowchart of do-while

In the Pretest loop initialization expression executes first and then executes an action, updates statements, and then checks the condition and the loop will iterate until and unless the condition is false.

The king point is initialization expression executes only once.

Updating expression :

In the loop, the update expression will change or update the value of the initialization expression at every iteration until and unless the condition is false

Example program to illustrate Initialization and Updating :

```
#include<stdio.h>
main( )
{
int i =1;//Initialization Expression
while( i < =10)
{
printf("%d",i);
i++; //Update Expression
}
}
main( )
{
for( int i =1; i< =5;i++)
{
printf("%d",i);
}
```

7. EVENT AND COUNTER CONTROLLED LOOPS :

1. *Event Controlled Loop*

*The programmer does not have any idea about how many times the loop is repeated until an event occurs.

*This is also called an indefinite repetition loop

Example program that illustrates Event controlled loop

```
#include<stdio.h>
main( )
{
int n;
```

```
printf("Enter n value between 5 to 20");
scanf("%d",&n);
while(n > = 5&& n< 20)
{
printf("%d",n);
printf("Enter n value between 5 to 20");
scanf("%d",&n);
}
}
```

In the above program, the programmer does not know when the while loop will get false.

The termination of the loop depends upon the end-user it's not in the hands of the programmer

2. *Counter controlled loop*

*The programmer has any idea about how many times the loop is iterated.

*In this loop, there is a variable called the looping variable or counter variable.

Procedure for Counter-controlled loop.

1. The initialization of a counter variable

2. Condition on the success it executes the body of the loop and then updates the counter variable.

The above steps are repeated until the condition is false.

It is also called definite loop repetition

Example program that illustrates counter controlled loop

```
#include<stdio.h>
main( )
{
int i =1; //Counter Variable
s = 0;
while(i <=10)
{
s = s+i;
i++; //Update Statement
}
printf("Sum is %d",s);
```

}

In the above program, the programmer knows when the while loop test condition is false that is loop iterates 10 times.

8. STATEMENTS RELATED TO LOOPING :

Jump Statements:

We know that execution flow in c language is top to bottom. Here jump statements play a key role in c language.

In case compiler evaluates the jump statements in c programmer then it terminates the normal flow.

C language consists of mainly 3 types.

- break Statement
- continue Statement
- goto Statement

break Statement:

In case the compiler executes the break statement on the spot the control the loop or switch statement ends and control executes the statements next to loop or switch statements.

Example 1:

An example program for working on a break statement in for loop.

Program:

```
#include<stdio.h>
void main()
{
int p; for(p=1;p<=6;p++)
{
if(p==4)
{
break;
```

```
}
else
{
printf("%d\t", p);
}
}
printf("\nAfter the for loop");
}
```

Output:

1 2 3
After the for loop

Explanation:

Check the condition, i.e. if (p==4), if it is true, control executer break statement and control terminate the loop and executes print statement after the for loop print "After break statement". And control ignore to execute remaining 2 iteration out of 6

Example 2:

An example program for working on a break statement in while loop.

Program:

```
#include<stdio.h>
void main()
{
int p=1; while(p<=6)
{
if (p==4)
{
break;
}
else
{
printf("%d\t",p);
}
p++;
}
```

```
printf("\nAfter the while loop");
}
```

Output:

1 2 3
After the while loop

Explanation:

Check the condition, i.e. if (p= =4), if it is true, control executer break statement. After execution of the break statement the control comes out of the loopand execute the statement after the while loop and print"After the break statement ". Here control ignore to execute remaining 2 iterations out of 6.

Example 3:

An example program for working on a break statement in do-while loop.

Program:

```
#include<stdio.h>
void main()
{
int p=1;
do
{
if(p==4)
{
break;
}
else
{
printf("%d\t",p);
}
p++;
}while(p<=6);
printf("\nAfter the do-while loop");
}
```

Output:

1 2 3
After the do-while loop

Explanation:

Check the condition, i.e. if (p= =4), If it is true, the control execute the break statement.After the execution of the break statement the control comes out of the loop,

And execute the statement after the do-while loop and print "After the do-while loop", Here control ignores to executes remaining 2 iterations out of 6.

Example 4:

An example program for working on a break statement in switch statement.

Program:

```
#include <stdio.h>
void main()
{
int p=4;
switch(p)
{
case 1:printf("1"); break;
case 2:printf("2"); break;
case 3:printf("3"); break;
case 4:printf("4"); break;
case 5:printf("5"); break;
case 6:printf("6"); break;
default: printf("wrong entry");
}
printf("\nAfter the switch statement");
}
```

Output: 4
After the switch statement

Explanation:

Check the condition, i.e. switch (P), control check p=4 with all case values.P=4 match with case 4 and point the value "4" and next execute break statement, then controlgoes out of the switch statement and print “After the switch statement".

continue Statement:

The main difference between a break and continue is :

- The *break statement* terminates the loop whenever the control evaluates the break statement.
- Immediately after the execution of *continue statement*, the control jumps to the beginning of the loop omits the statement Safter continue statement.

Note: continue statement skips the iteration and control goes to the beginning of the loop.

Syntax:

continue;

Example 1:

An example program for working of continue statement in for loop.

Program:

```
#include<stdio.h>
void main()
{
int p; for(p=1;p<=6;p++)
{
if(p==4)
{
continue;
}
printf("%d\t", p);
}
}
```

Output: 1 2 3 5 6

Explanation:

After above program executes the output is **1 2 3 5 6** at iteration 4 the control executes continue statements and it omits the statement printf("%d\t", p) and control goes to update statement because of this control skips to print the value 4.

Example 2:

An example program for working of continue statement in while loop.

Program:

```
#include<stdio.h>
void main()
{
int p=1; while (p<=6)
{
if (p==4)
{
p++;
continue;
}
printf("%d\t", p); p++;
}
}
```

Output:

1 2 3 5 6

Explanation:

After the execution of the above program, the iteration 4 control executes update (p++) and continue statements and it omits the statements after the continue statements, i.e. printf("%d\t", p) and p++, because of this control cannot print the value 4.

goto Statement :

The goto statement used to transfer a control from one place to another place in a function. The goto statement permits to transfer a control to a particular label.

Syntax:

```
goto label;
--------
--------
label:
//statement;
```

Example 1:

Design a c program to print given number is even or odd using *goto* Statement.

Program:

```
#include<stdio.h>
int main()
{
int k;
printf("Enter k value\n"); scanf("%d", &k); if(k%2==0)
{
goto even_label;
}
else
{
goto odd_label;
}
even_label: printf("number is even"); return 0;
odd_label: printf("number is odd"); return 0;
}
```

Output:

```
Enter k value
5
number is odd
```

Enter k value
8
number is even

Explanation:

In the above program

1. Checks the condition, i.e., if (k%2==0).
2. If the condition is true the control executes the ***goto*** statement and the control jumps unconditionally to the particular identifier even: and executes the statements followed by the identifier even:
3. If the condition is false, then the control executes the ***goto*** statement in else block. And the control jumps unconditionally to a particular identifier odd: and executes the statements followed by identifier odd.

Example 2:

Design a c program to print 1 to k natural numbers using goto statement.

Program:

```
#include<stdio.h>
void main()
{
int k, p=1; printf("Enter k value");
scanf("%d", &k);
loop:
if (p<=k)
{
printf("%d\t", p); p++;
goto loop;
}
}
```

Output:

Enter k value 5
1 2 3 4 5

Explanation:

In the above program

Check the condition, i.e. if (p<=k), if the condition is true, the control executes the statements and the control jumps unconditionally to a particular identifier **loop:** This process continues until the condition is false.

III

ARRAYS,STRINGS, STRUCTURE AND UNIONS

CONTENTS : Arrays: One-dimensional array, Two Dimensional Arrays, Applications of Arrays Strings: String Concepts, String Input / Output Functions, Arrays of Strings, String Manipulation Functions String/ Data Conversion, A Programming Example – Morse Code Enumerated, Structure, Array of Structures, Structure using pointers, nested structure and Union: The Type Definition (Type def), Structure, Unions.

1. ARRAYS

- Arrays mean which holds the same /homogeneous data in continuous memory.
- It is called derived data type.

1. One-Dimensional Array
Declaration:

data type array-name [size];
Example:
1. int p [5]:- The array variable p can store 5 values of type integers only.

Assume the memory allocation of int p[5]
2. float p [5]:-The array variable p can store 5 values of type floating-point values only
Assume the memory allocation of float p[5]

Pivotal points of an array are:
Array variable holds starting address of an array.

- Array variable *is starting* index 0 and *ending* index is n-1.
  Ex: -If the array size is 5, here starting index is 0, and the ending *index* is 4.
- Every index has a corresponding address. For example, if it is an integer array, assume the size of the int is 2 bytes.

Initialization :

Static Initialization:

On static initialization, array initialization happens at compile -time
Syntax:-
data type array _name [size]={value1, value2, ...value n-1};

Example :

int p [5] ={11, 24, 29, 48, 13};
float f [5] ={11.5, 24.3, 29.4, 48.22, 13.67};
char c [5] ={'x', 'd', 'R', 'K', 'Y'};

Dynamic Initialization :

On dynamic initialization, array initialization happens at runtime, by using the scanf () function.

```
main()
{
int p [5]; //array declaration printf(" Enter array values"); for (int
k=0;k<=4;k++)
{
scan f ("%d", &p[k]); //array initialization at run-time
}
}
```

Accessing :

By using an array index, we can access values in an array. Here array has n elements, index 0 is the starting index and index n-1 is the last index.

For example :

int p [5]={11, 24, 29, 48, 13};

Here p is the array variable

Pictorial representation of an above array

We have two ways to access array of elements

Access Array Values Without Using a Loop (1st way):-

Printf ("%d\n", p[0]); // print value at index.0, i.e. 11
Printf ("%d\n", p[1]); // print value at index 1, i.e. 24
Printf ("%d\n", p[2]); // print value at index 2, i.e. 29
Printf ("%d\n", p[3]); // print value at index 3, i.e. 48
Printf ("%d\n", p[4]); // printvalue at index 4, i.e. 13

Access Array Values Using a Loop (2nd way) :

for (int k=0; k<=4; k++)
{
Print f ("%d\t", p[k]); // print the value of array p at index k.
}

When do we need an array?

The normal variable holds a single value and whereas an array variable holds one or more values. If there is a situation to store one or more values, then go with arrays.

Let us consider a scenario to store the first 10 patients' temperatures in a hospital.

Without Using Arrays :

Declare 10 patient variables to store temperature

float patient1, patient2, patient3, patient4, patient5, patient6, patient7, patient8, patient9, patient10;

patient1=98.2, patient2=99, patient3=97.68,
patient4=98, patient5=100, patient6=101,
patient7=99, patient8=98.5, patient9=101,

patient10=100;

From the above example, we understand that need to declare 10 variables to store the temperature of 10 patients. In case we have to store the temperature of 100 patients then we have to declare 100 variables. So, in this case, it is difficult to declare 100 variables. To overcome the above drawback we are going to use an array.

With Using an Array:

Declare an array variable of a size 10 to store temperature of patients.

float p[10]={98.2, 99, 97.68, 98, 100, 101, 99, 98.5, 101,100};

From the above example, we understand that no nto eed declare 10 variables to store temperature of 10 patients, simply give the array as 10. In case we want to store the temperature of 100 patients then we have to change the size of the array to 100.

Example Programs:

1. Design a program

- **Setup an array of size k (holds k integer)**
- **Read the data into an array at run-time**
- **Print the sum of the elements in an array**

Program:

```
# include<stdio.h>
void main()
{
int k, s, sum_val=0; printf("Enter size of an array");
scanf ("%d", &k);
int p[k];
printf("Enter elements into an array");
for(s=0;s<k;s++)
{
scanf("%d", &p[s]);
}
// calculate the sum of elements in an array for(s=0;s<k;s++)
{
sum_val=sum_val+p[s];
```

```
}
// print sum of elements in an array printf("Sum is %d", sum_val);
}
```

Output :

Enter size of an array4
Enter elements into an array2 4 2 9
Sum is 17

Explanation :

In the above program

1. Read k value to store k elements in an array.
2. Repeat the for loop to read the elements into an array on run-time.
3. Again, repeat the for loop to fetch an array element to do the sum of all elements.
4. Print the sum.

2. Design a c program,

Set up an array of size k
Read the data into an array at run-time
Print the even numbers in an array

Program :

```
#include <stdio.h> void main()
{
int k, s;
printf("Enter the size of an array:"); scanf("%d", &k);
int p[k];
printf("Enter elements into an array:"); for(s=0;s<k;s++)
{
scanf("%d", &p[s]);
}
// print even numbers in an array
//print("even numbers in an array are"); for(s=0;s<k;s++)
{
if(p[s]%2==0)
{
printf("%d\t", p[s]);
}
```

```
}
}
```

Output :

Enter the size of an array:6
Enter elements into an array:3 6 5 2 4 9
6 2 4

Explanation :

1. Read value to store k elements into an array.
2. Repeat the for loop to read the elements into an array at array run-time.
3. Again, repeat the for loop and check every element in an array is even or not if it is even, then prints that number otherwise not.

3) Design a c program

- **Setup an array of size k**
- **Read the data into an array and run time**
- **Print the largest value in an array**

Program :

```
#include <stdio.h>
void main()
{
int k, s, large_val;
printf("Enter size of an array:");
scanf("%d", &k);
int p[k];
printf("Enter elements into an array:");
for(s=0;s<k;s++)
{
scanf("%d", &p[s]);
}
large_val=p[0];
//print large value in an array for(s=1;s<k;s++)
{
if(large_val<p[s])
{
```

```
large_val=p[s];
}
}
printf("Large_value is:%d", large_val);
}
```

Output :

Enter the size of an array:2
Enter elements into an array:7 8 Large_value is:8

Explanation :

1. Read k value to store k elements in an array.
2. Repeat the for loop to read the elements into an array at run-time
3. Setlarge_val=p [0], (starting element in an array).4.
4. Again, repeat the for loop and check the condition if (large_val<p[s]) then updated large_val with p [s] do the above process up to loop breaks.
5. Finally, the print value in large_val is the largest value.

4) Design a C program

- **Setup 2 arrays of size k1 and k2 respectively**
- **Read the data into those 2 arrays at run-time**
- **Print the array after merging the 2 arrays**

Program :

```
#include <stdio.h>
void main()
{
int k1, k2, s1, s2, p[100], y[100], merge[100];
printf("Enter the size of array1 & array2_:");
scanf("%d %d", &k1, &k2);
printf("Enter elements into an array-1_:");
for(s1=0;s1<k1;s1++)
{
scanf("%d", &p[s1]);
}
printf("Enter elements into an array-2_:");
```

```
for(s2=0;s2<k2;s2++)
{
scanf("%d", &y[s2]);
}
//copy elements in array p to array merge
for(s1=0;s1<k1;s1++)
{
merge[s1]=p[s1];
}
//copy elements in array p to array merge
for(s2=0;s2<k2;s2++)
{
merge[s1]=y[s2];
s1++;
}
//print elements in an array merge
//printf("elements after merge");
for(s1=0;s1<(k1+k2);s1++)
{
printf("%d\t", merge[s1]);
}
}
```

Output:

Enter the size of array1 & array2_:3 4 Enter elements into an array-1_:1 2 3 Enter elements into an array-2_:4 5 6 7
1 2 3 4 5 6 7

Explanation:

1. Read k1 and k2 values.
2. Repeat the for loop to read the elements in an array p [100]and y [100] at run-time.
3. Repeat the for loop to copy elements in an array p[100] to an array merge [100].
4. Again, repeat the for loop the copy elements in an array y [100] into an array merge [100] (from previous elements).
5. Print the elements in an array merge [100] on the screen.

2. Two- Dimensional Array :

The 2-D array looks like a binding up of two or more 1-D arrays in a single unit. It is nothing but a matrix, which contains rows and columns. It is the simplest form of a multi dimensional array.

A 2-D array means which holds same/homogeneous data in a contiguous memory with two subscript variables. First subscript for "Row" and second subscript for "Column" of a matrix.

Declaration :

datatype array_name[row_size][col_size];

Here row_size is first subscript and col_size is second subscript.

Example :

int P[3][3];

It is nothing but 3 x 3matrix. The array variable p has a capacity to store 9 values of type integers only.

Let us assume memory allocation of int P[3][3].

Here P[0][0], P[0][1], P[0][2], P[1][0]... are nothing but P[row_index][column_index]and 2000, 2002, 2004,

2006, 2008, 2010, 2012, 2014, 2016 are addressed of a particular memory location.

Note: Here values are stored in a contiguous memory location.

Pivotal Points Of 2-D Array :

1. Array variable holds starting address of an 2-D array.
2. In 2-D Array variable, starting row index and column index is 0 and ending row index and column index is row_size-1 and column_size-1 respectively. For example, if array size is 4 x 3, here starting row index and column index is 0 and ending row index and column index is 3 and 2 respectively.

Here data stored in a contiguous memory location. For example, if it is an integer array, then the size of an integer is 2 bytes.

Initialization :

1) Static Initialization:

On static initialization, array initialization happens at compile-time. (manually)

Syntax :

1st method :

```
int P[3][3] = {{10, 22, 24},
{44, 15, 71},
{27, 48, 39}};
```

2nd method :

```
int P[3][3] = {10, 22, 24, 44, 15, 71, 27, 48, 39};
```

Assume memory allocation for above matrix int P[3][3].

2) Dynamic Initialization :

On dynamic initialization, array initialization happens at run-time, by using scanf() function.

Syntax :

```
#include <stdio.h>
void main()
{
int P[3][3]; // 2-D Array declaration
printf("Enter values into the Array\n");
for(int m=0; m<3; m++)
{
for(int k=0; k<3; k++)
{
scanf("%d ", &P[m][k]);
}
}
}
```

Accessing :

By using row index and column index we can access the elements in the 2-D array.

Example:

```
int P[3][3] = {{2, 4, 8}, {2, 9, 6}, {13, 8, 7}};
```

Here P is array variable.

We have two ways to access 2-D array elements.

1) Accessing 2-D Array Values Without Using a Loop (1st way) :

```
printf("%d ", P[0][0]); // print value at index 00, i.e. 2
printf("%d ", P[0][1]); // print value at index 01, i.e. 4
printf("%d ", P[0][2]); // print value at index 02, i.e. 8
printf("%d ", P[1][0]); // print value at index 10, i.e. 2
printf("%d ", P[1][1]); // print value at index 11, i.e. 9
printf("%d ", P[1][2]); // print value at index 12, i.e. 6
printf("%d ", P[2][0]); // print value at index 20, i.e. 13
printf("%d ", P[2][1]); // print value at index 21, i.e. 8
printf("%d ", P[2][2]); // print value at index 22, i.e. 7
```

2) Accessing 2-D Array Values Using a Loop (2nd way) :

```
for(int d=0; d<=2; d++)
{
for(int k=0; k<=2; k++)
{
printf("%d\t", p[d][k]);
}
printf("\n");
}
```

Output :

2 4 8

2 9 6

13 8 7

Here variable 'd' represents the row and 'k' represents a column.

Example Programs :

1) Design a program

- **Setup a 2-D array with row size 3 and column size 3.**
- **Read the data into a 2-D array at run-time.**
- **Print the sum and product of the elements in a 2-D array(matrix)**

Program :

```
#include<stdio.h>
void main()
```

```
{
int p[3][3], d, k, s=0, product=1;
printf("Enter the data into 2-D array\n");
for(d=0; d<=2; d++)
{
for(k=0; k<=2; k++)
{
scanf("%d", &p[d][k]);
}
}
//print sum and product of the elements in a 2-D array
for(d=0; d<=2; d++)
{
for(k=0; k<=2; k++)
{
s=s + p[d][k];
product=product * p[d][k];
}
}
printf("Sum of values in 2-D array is:\n %d\n", s);
printf("Product of values in 2-D array is:\n %d\n", product);
}
```

Output:

Enter the data into a 2-D array 1 2 3 4 5 6 7 8 9
Sum of values in a 2-D array is :
45
Product of values in the 2-D array is :
362880

Explanation:

In the above program

1. We read the values into a 3 x 3 matrix by using outer and inner for loops. Here outer for loop indicates the row number and the inner for loop indicates column number.
2. Calculate the sum and product of values in a 3 x 3 matrix by using outer and inner for loops.

3. Print sum and product values on the screen.

2) Design a program

- **Set up a two 2-D array with row size 3 and column size 3.**
- **Read the data into 2-D arrays at run-time.**

Print addition of two 2-D arrays(matrix)

Program:

```
#include<stdio.h>
main()
{
int res[3][3], d[3][3], p[3][3], s, k;
printf("Enter 1st matrix\n");
//read data into 2-D array d[3][3]
for(s=0; s<=2; s++)
{
for(k=0; k<=2; k++)
{
scanf("%d ", &d[s][k]);}
}
printf("Enter 2nd matrix\n");
//read data into 2-D array, i.e. P[3][3]
for(s=0; s<=2; s++)
{
for(k=0; k<=2; k++)
{
scanf("%d ", &p[s][k]);
}
}
//addittion of two matrices(2-D arrays)
for(s=0; s<=2; s++)
{
for(k=0; k<=2; k++)
{
res[s][k]= d[s][k] + p[s][k];
}
```

```
}
}
//print resultant matrix
printf("Addition of two matrices are:\n");
for(s=0; s<=2; s++)
{
for(k=0; k<=2; k++)
{
printf("%d\t", res[s][k]);
}
printf("\n");
}
}
```

Output:

Enter 1st matrix
1 2 3 4 5 6 7 8
9
Enter 2nd matrix
2 3 4 1 5 6 4 2
21
The addition of two matrices are:
3 5 7
5 10 12
11 10 30

Explanation:

|In the above program

1. We have read the values of 2 (3 x 3) matrices by using outer and inner for loops. Here outer for loop indicates the row number and the inner for loop indicates the column number.
2. Add d[row_number][column_number] and p[row_number][column_number] and store in res[row_number][column_number] by using outer and
3. inner for loops. Here outer for loop indicates the row number and the inner for loop indicates the column number.
4. Print resultant matrix by using outer and inner for loop.

3) Design a program

- **Setup a 2-D array (matrix) with row size 3 and column size 3**
- **Read the data into a 2-D array (matrix)at run-time.**
- **Print the sum of diagonal elements in a 2-D array(matrix)**

Program:

```
#include<stdio.h>
void main()
{
int p[3][3], d, k, sum_val=0;
printf("Enter the data into 2-D array\n");
for(d=0; d<=2; d++)
{
for(k=0; k<=2; k++)
{
scanf("%d", &p[d][k]);
}
}
for(d=0; d<=2; d++)
{
for(k=0; k<=2; k++)
{
if(d==k)
{
sum_val=sum_val+p[d][k];
}
}
}
printf("Sum of diagonal elements in a 2-D array:\n%d", sum_val);
}
```

Output:

```
Enter the data into a 2-D array
5 4 3 6 7 8 9 12 5
Sum of diagonal elements in a 2-D array:
17
```

Explanation:

In the above program

1. We read the values into a 3 x 3 matrix by using outer and inner for loop. Here outer for loop indicates the row number and the inner for loop indicates column number.
2. Repeat the loops, if outer for loop number equals to inner for loop number, then, sum_val = sum_val + p[row_number][column_number].
3. Print sum_val on screen.

Note: If row number and column number are the same then it is a diagonal element.

4) Design a program

- **Setup a 2-D array(matrix) with row size 3 and column size 3.**
- **Read the data into a 2-D array(matrix) at run-time.**
- **Print lthe ower matrix of a given 2-D array(matrix).**

Program:

```
#include<stdio.h>
void main()
{
int p[3][3], d, k;
printf("Enter data into 2-D array\n");
for(d=0; d<=2; d++)
{
for(k=0; k<=2; k++)
{
scanf("%d", &p[d][k]);
}
}
//print the given matrix
printf("Print the given matrix\n");
for(d=0; d<=2; d++)
{
for(k=0; k<=2; k++)
```

```
{
printf("%d\t", p[d][k]);
}
printf("\n");
}
//print lower matrix
printf("Lower matrix of a given matrix\n");
for(d=0; d<=2; d++)
{
for(k=0; k<=2; k++)
{
if(d>=k)
{
printf("%d\t", p[d][k]);
}
else
{
printf("%d\t", 0);
}
}
printf("\n");
}
}
```

Output :

Enter data into 2-D array
43 54 67 91 94 23 11 45
12
Print the given matrix 43 54 67
91 94 23
11 45 12
Lower matrix of a given matrix 43 0 0
91 94 0
11 45 12

Explanation :

In the above program

1. We read values into a 3 x 3 matrix by using the outer loop and inner loop. Here outer loop indicates the row number and the inner loop indicates the column number.
2. Print the given matrix by using outer and inner for loop.
3. Repeat the loops, if the row number is greater than or equals to the column number (d>=k) then print p[d][k]

   i.e. d is a row number and k is the column number, otherwise print 0.

2. APPLICATIONS OF ARRAYS :

- *Array are used in mathematical problems like matrices etc.*
- *Arrays are used in data structure. Array are used to store list of similar values.*
- *Arrays are used for sorting elements*
- *Arrays are used for searching elements*
- *Arrays are used for CPU scheduling rays are used for a stack and queue*

3. STRINGS :

Introduction to Strings

"" Strings are nothing but a 1-D character array ending with a null character '\0' "."

Syntax Declaration : *char string_name [size];*

Here string_name is the name of the character array and size is the size of the character array.

Example:

char std_name [20];

Here std_name is the name of the character array and 20 is the size of the character array.

String Input/Output Functions :

1. Initialization Static Initialization :

- char std_name[8] = " koti ";
- char std_name[] = " Koti" ;
- 3. char std_name [8] = {'k', 'o', 't', 'i', '\0' };
- 4. char std_name[] = {"K', 'o', 't', 'i', \0'};

In *char std_name [20]="koti"*, compiler inserts null character '\0' automatically.

Case Study- With Null Character:

Case-1 : *char std_name [8]={'k', 'o', 't', 'i', '\0'};*

Here the size of character array std_name is 8, i.e. 8 bytes of memory will allocate. If we try to execute the statement, *printf ("%s", std_name);* the compiler prints the string up to the null character '\0' and the output is 'koti'.The Null Character '\0' does not permit the compiler to execute after '\0'.

Note: *Compiler stops printing the character after the Null Character '\0'.*

2 . Dynamic Initialization:

By using the scanf()and gets () function, we can initialize the character array dynamically.

Using Scanf( ) :

```
#include <stdio.h>
void main ()
```

```
{
char std_name [20];
printf ("Enter Student Name: ");
scanf ("%s\n", std_name);
printf ("\nName is: %s", std_name);
}
```

Output 1:

Enter Student Name: Koti Name is: Koti

Output 2:

Enter Student Name: Koti Mani Kumar Name is: Koti

Explanation:

In the above program,

1. Declare character array, i.e. char std_name [20].
2. Read data by using scanf ()function.Thescanf () function reads a single word only, i.e., scanf () function ignores the word or string after the space.

Using gets ( ):

```
#include <stdio.h>
void main ()
{
char std_name [20];
printf ("Enter student name:"); gets (std_name);
printf ("Name is:%s", std_name);
}
```

Output 1:

Enter Student Name: Koti Name is: Koti

Output 2:

Enter Student Name: Koti Mani Kumar Name is: Koti Mani Kumar

Explanation:

In the above program,

1. Declare character array, i.e. char std-name [20].
2. Read the data by using gets ()function.The gets () function reads the whole sentence. The gets () function obeys the word after the space.

Accessing

By using puts () and printf () function, we can access the data in character array.

Syntax:

printf ("%s ", character_arrayName); puts (character_arrayName);

Using printf()

```
#include<stdio.h>
void main ()
{
char std_name [20];
printf ("Enter Student Name:");
gets (std_name);
printf ("Name is:%s", std_name); //accessing
}
```

Output :

Enter Student Name: Koti Mani Kumar
Name is: Koti Mani Kumar

Using puts ()

```
#include<stdio.h>
void main ()
{
char std_name [20];
printf ("Enter Student Name:");
gets (std_name);
puts (std_name); //accessing character array
}
```

Output :

Enter Student Name: Koti Mani Kumar
Name is: Koti Mani Kumar

String Manipulation Functions

All string manipulation/handling functions works under the ***#include <string.h>*** standard library.

Some String Handling Functions are:

1. strlen ()
2. strcat ()
3. strcmp ()
4. strcpy ()

1. String Length (strlen ()):

The ***strlen ()*** function gives the length of a string.

(Or)

It returns the count of the number of characters in a string.

Syntax:

int str_len= strnlen (string);

Example :

An Example program to illustrate the strlen () function. Program:

```
#include<stdio.h>
#include<string.h>
void main ()
{
int str_len;
char city [20]="Amalapuram"; str_len =strlen (city);
printf ("The Length of the string city is:%d", str_len);
}
```

Output :

The Length of the string city is:10

2. String Concatenation (strcat ()):

The ***strcat ()*** function, attaches one string to another.

Syntax:

strcat (first-string, second_string);

strcat () function concatenates or appends second-string to first-string.

Example: An example program to illustrate strcat () function.

Program :

```
#include<stdio.h>
#include<string.h>
main ()
{
```

```
char first_string [100] ="Koti " ;
char second_string [100] = "Mani Kumar ";
strcat (first_string, second_string);
printf ("After Concatenation First String: %s", first_string);
}
```

Output :

After Concatenation First String: Koti Mani Kumar

3. String Compare (strcmp ()) :

The ***strcmp ()*** function, compares two strings,

1. If strcmp () function returns 0, denotes that two strings are same.
2. If strcmp () function returns -1, denotes that first string less than the second string.
3. If strcmp () function returns 1, denotes that first string greater than the second string.

Syntax:

int return_val = strcmp (first_string, second_string);

Example:

```
#include<stdio.h>
#include<string.h>
void main ()
{
char first_string [100], second_string [100] ;
printf ("Enter First String:");
scanf ("%s\n", first_string); printf ("Enter Second String:");
scanf ("%s\n", second_string);
int return_val=strcmp (first_string, second_string);
if (return_val==0)
{
printf (" Both Are Same. ");
}
else if ( return_val< 0)
{ printf (" First String is less than Second String");
}
else
{
```

```
printf ("First string is greater than second string ");
}
}
```

Output 1 :

Enter First String: koti Enter Second String: koti Both Are Same

Output 2 :

Enter First String: koti

Enter Second String: manikumar First String is less than Second String

Output 3 :

Enter First String: Mani kumar Enter Second String: Koti

First String is less than Second String

4. String Copy (strcpy())

The ***strcpy ()*** function, copies second string to the first string.

Syntax :

strcpy (first_string, second_string);

An Example program to illustrate strcpy () function

Program :

```
#include<stdio.h>
#include<string.h>
void main ()
{
char first_string [100] ;
char second_string [100] = "Mani Kumar ";
strcpy (first_string, second_string);
printf ("After Copy First String Is: %s", first_string);
}
```

Output :

After Copy First String Is: Mani Kumar

Example Programs on Strings Without Using String Handling Functions

Example 1 :

Design a program to find the length of a given string, Without using strlen () function.

Program :

```
#include<stdio.h>
void main ()
{
int p, str_count = 0;
char first_string[30];
printf("Enter a string: ");
gets (first_string );
for ( p = 0; first_string [p]!='\0'; p++ )
{
str_count ++;
}
printf ("Length of the string: %d ", str_count );
}
```

Output:

Enter a string: Koti
Length of the string: 4

Explanation:

In the above program,

1. Declare a string first_string[30].
2. Repeat a loop and increment a str_count until the element at character array first_string [p] equals to null character '\0'.
3. Print the length ofstring, i.e.str_count.

Example 2:

An example program to concatenate two strings without using strcat () function.

Program:

```
#include<stdio.h>
void main ()
{
int c_val =0, s1;
char first_string [100], second_string [100];
printf ( "Enter first and second strings: ");
scanf (" %s %s ", first_string, second_string);
// To find the length of first string.
for ( s1= 0 ; first_string [s1]!='\0'; s1++)
{
```

```
c_val++;
}
// To append second_string to first_string. for ( s1=0; second_string [s1]!='\0' ;s1++)
{
first_string[c_val] = second_string [s1]; c_val++ ;
}
first_string [c_val] ='\0';
printf ("After concatenation string is: %s", first_string );
}
```

Output:

Enter first and second strings: Koti Mani

After concatenation string is: KotiMani

Explanation:

In the above program,

1. Declare first_string [100], second_string [100].
2. Read data in two strings.
3. Find the length of the string, i.e. char first_string [100] and store the count in c_val.
4. Repeat a loop to append second_string to first_string from first_string [c_val], and then increment c_val until second_string [s1]! ='\0'.
5. Print first_string after append.

Example 3 :

An Example program to compare two strings without using strcmp () function?

Program :

```
#include<stdio.h>
#include<string.h>
void main ()
{
int s1, s2, flag =0;
char first_string [100], second_string [100];
printf ("Enter first string: ");
scanf ("%s \n", first_string);
printf ("Enter secondstring: ");
scanf ("%s \n", second_string);
```

```
int len_str1 = strlen (first_string);
int len_str2 = strlen (second_string);
if ( len_str1 == len_str2)
{
for ( s1 =0;first_string [s1]!='\0';s1++)
{
if (first_string [s1] == second_string [s2])
{
continue;
}
else
{
flag=1;
break;
}
}
}
else
{
flag=1;
}
if ( flag ==0 )
{
printf (" Two strings are same ");
}
else
{
printf ("Two strings are not same");
}
}
```

Output 1:

Enter first string: Koti
Enter secondstring: Koti
Two strings are same

Output 2:

Enter first string: Koti
Enter secondstring: Mani
Two strings are not same

Explanation:

In the above program,

1. Read the data into two strings.
2. Calculate lengths of two strings, if length of two strings is same not, then printing "Two strings are not same". If length of two strings is same thengotostep3.
3. Repeat the for loop and compare each and every character from two strings until the condition is false.
4. If all the characters from two strings are same then print "Two strings are same" otherwise print: "Two strings are not same".

Example 4 :

An example to copy one string to another without using strcpy (), function.

Program :

```
#include<stdio.h>
#include<string.h>
void main ()
{
int s1;
char first_string [100], second_string [100];
printf ("Enter first string: ");
scanf ("%s \n", first_string);
for ( s1=0; second_string [s1]!='\0' ;s1++)
{
second_string [s1]= first_string [s1] ;
}
printf ("After copy the second string is: %s", second_string);
}
```

Output:

Enter first string: Koti

After copy the second string is: Koti

Explanation :

In the above program,

1. Declare char first_string[100], second_string [100], and character arrays.
2. Read data into first_string.

3. Repeat the loop and copy every character in first_string to second_string until the condition of the loop is false.
4. Print "After copy the string is: Koti" on the screen.

Array of Strings

Array of strings is nothing but two-dimensional character array.

Syntax – declaration:

char array_Name [Row_size] [Column_size];

Here row size indicates number of strings and column size indicates number of characters in a string.

Initialisation:

1st way :

char array_Name[4] [10] = { "koti","mani","kumar","kiran" };

2nd way :

char array_name[4][10]={{'k', 'o', 't', 'i', '\0'},{'m', 'a', 'n', 'i', '\0'},{'k', 'u', 'm', 'a', 'r','\0'},{'k', 'i', 'r', 'a', 'n', '\0'}};

Here row size is 4 and column size is 10, means that 4 rows and each row has capacity to store 10 characters. Above

two dimensional characters array holds 4(rows)*(columns) = 40 characters(40 bytes of memory).

Assume the address should be like this

Different Methods to Solve Programs on Array Of Strings:

Method-1 :

```
/* A"C" program to initialize a 2-D Array of characters*/
#include <stdio.h>
int main()
{
char array_name[4][10]={"koti", "mani", "kumar", "kiran"};
for(int p=0;p<4;p++)
{
printf("%s\n", array_name+p);
```

```
}
return 0;
}
```

Output: koti
mani
kumar
kiran

Method-2 :

/* A"C" program to initialize a 2-D Array of characters*/

```
#include <stdio.h>
int main()
{char array_name[4][10]={ {'k', 'o', 't', 'i', '\0'},{'m', 'a', 'n', 'i', '\0'},{'k', 'u', 'm', 'a',
'r', '\0'},{'k', 'i', 'r', 'a', 'n', '\0'} };
for(int p=0;p<4;p++)
{
printf("%s\n", array_name [p]);
/* We can use array_name [p] instead of array_name +pat print statement.
*/
}
return 0;
}
```

Output:
koti
mani
kumar
kiran

Method: 3 (By using 2 for loops)

/* A"C" program to initialize a 2-D Array of characters using "2 for loops"*/

```
#include <stdio.h>
int main()
{
char array_name[4][10]={"koti", "mani", "kumar", "kiran"};
for(int p=0;p<4;p++)
{
for(int q=0;array_name[p][q]!='\0';q++)
```

```
{
printf("%c", array_name[p][q]);
}
printf("\n");
}
return 0;
}
```

Output:
koti
mani
kumar
kiran

4. MORSE CODE

```
#include <stdio.h>
int main()
{
int i;
char a[100]="sir crr";
for(i=0;a[i]!='\0';i++)
{
switch (a[i])
{
case 'a':
printf("%s ", ".-"); break;
case 'b':
printf("%s ", "-...");break;
case 'c':
printf("%s ", "-.-.");break;
case 'd':
printf("%s ", "-..");break;
case 'e':
printf("%s ", ".");break;
case 'f':
printf("%s ", "..-.");break;
case 'g':
printf("%s ", "--.");break;
```

```
case 'h':
printf("%s ", "....");break;
case 'i':
printf("%s ", "..");break;
case 'j':
printf("%s ", ".---");break;
case 'k':
printf("%s ", "-.-");break;
case 'l':
printf("%s ", ".-..");break;
case 'm':
printf("%s ", "--");break;
case 'n':
printf("%s ", "-.");break;
case 'o':
printf("%s ", "---");break;
case 'p':
printf("%s ",".--.");break;
case 'q':
printf("%s ", "--.-");break;
case 'r':
printf("%s ", ".-.");break;
case 's':
printf("%s ", "...");break;
case 't':
printf("%s ", "-");break;
case 'u':
printf("%s ", "..-");break;
case 'v':
printf("%s", "...-");break;
case 'w':
printf("%s ", ".--");break;
case 'x':
printf("%s ", "-..-");break;
case 'y':
printf("%s ", "-.--");break;
case 'z':
printf("%s ", "--..");break;
```

```
case '1':
printf("%s ", ".----");break;
case '2':
printf("%s ", "..---");break;
case '3':
printf("%s ", "...--");break;
case '4':
printf("%s ", "....-");break;
case '5':
printf("%s ", ".....");break;
case '6':
printf("%s ", "-....");break;
case '7':
printf("%s ", "--...");break;
case '8':
printf("%s ","---..");break;
case '9':
printf("%s ", "----.");break;
case '0':
printf("%s ","-----");break;
case ' ':
printf("%s ","/");break;
default:
printf("Found invalid character");
}
}
return 0;
}
```

Output : ... .. .-. / -.-. .-. .-.

5. STRUCTURE AND UNION :

Introduction to Structures

Structure is a user defined data type, which is used to store data with different types.

For Example:

If we want to store patient details like patient_id, patient_Name, patient_age, and disease name etc.. We can use structures, because structure holds different data types in a single unit.

Structure Definition :

struct<structure_Name>

[datatype member1; datatype member2;

.

.

.

datatype member n;

];

Example of structure Definition :-

struct patient_Details

[

int patient_id;

char patient_Name[20]; int age;

char disease[20]; float fee;

];

- Here we can use struct keyword followed by a structure name.
- Structure name should not be any C keyword and follow the rules of identifier.
- Structure members are of mixed type or the same type.
- Structure definition should end with semicolon(;).
- Above Structure definition contains different types of data types like int, char, and float.
- Memory should not allocate at the time of Structure definition.

Declaration of Structure Variable

Here we have two possibilities to declare a structure variable.

1. Declaration of structure variable with Structure definition.
2. Declaration of structure variable outside the Structure definition.

- *Whenever a structure variable is declared, then only memory is allocated to structure members, but not at structure definition.*

Declaration of Structure Variable With Structure Definition :

Here there is a provision to declare a structure variable along with structure definition. i.e., declare a structure variable next to close bracket (}) of structure definition and before the semicolon(;) of the structure definition.

Syntax :

```
struct<structure_Name>
{ datatype member 1;
datatype member 2;
.
.
datatype member n;
} var1, var2,....... var n;
```

Example:

```
struct patient_Details
{
int patient_id;
char patient_Name[20]; int age;
char disease[20]; float fee;
}pd1, pd2;
```

- Whenever the compiler executes the structure variable pd1, pd2 then only memory allocation done for member variables or fields of a structure based on structure padding concept.

Declaration Of Structure Variable Outside the Structure Definition:-

Here we have another provision to declare a structure variable outside the structure definition, i.e., declare a structure variable inside a main() function.

Syntax :

```
struct<structure_Name>
{ datatype member 1;
datatype member 2;
.
```

```
.
datatype member n;
};
main()
{
struct<structure_Name>var1, var2;
}
```

Example :

```
struct patient_Details
{
int patient_id;
char patient_Name[20]; int age;
char disease[20]; int fee;
};
void main()
{
struct patient_Details pd1, pd2;
}
```

Initialization of Structure Members

In order to initialize structure members, dot (.) operator should be used.

Structure Definition:

```
struct patient_Details
{
int patient_id;
char patient_Name[20]; int age;
char disease[20]; float fee;
};
```

1st Way (Initialize at Compile Time) :

Syntax:

```
struct<structure_Name>variable_Name={value 1, value 2,..... value n};
```

Example:

```
main()
{
structpatient_Details pd1={1, "xyz", 28, "covid19", 40000};
}
```

Here value 1 store in patient_id, "xyz" stores in patient_Name, 28 stores in age, "covid19"stores in disease and 40000 stores in fee variables.

2nd Way(Initialize at Compile Time):

Syntax :

struct<structure_Name>variable_Name; variable_Name.structure member=value;

Example:

```
main()
{
struct patient_Details pd1;
pd1.patient_id=1;
pd1.patient_Name="xyz"; pd1.age=28;
pd1.disease="covid19";
pd1.fee=40000;
}
```

3rd way(Initialize at Run Time) :

Syntax:

scanf("format specifier", &structure variable.structure member);

Example:

```
main()
{
struct patient_Details pd1;
printf("Enter patient id");
scanf("%d\n", pd1.patient_id);
printf("Enter patient Name");
scanf("%s\n", pd1.patient_Name);
printf("Enter age");
scanf("%d\n", &pd1.age); printf("Enter disease");
scanf("%s\n", pd1.disease); printf("Enter fee");
scanf("%f\n", &pd1.fee);
}
```

Here we can initialize the values at run time by using dot(.) operators, i.e. Structure variable. Structure member.

Accessing Structure Members

In order to access structure members, dot(.) operator should be used.

Syntax :

structure _variable.structure_member;

Example :

```
#include<stdio.h>
#include<string.h>
struct patient_Details
{
int patient_id;
char patient_Name[20]; int age;
char disease[20]; float fee;
};
int main()
{
struct patient_Details pd1={1, "xyz", 28, "covid19", 40000};
//Accessing structure members printf("patient id is %d\n", pd1.patient_id);
printf("patient Name: %s\n", pd1.patient_Name);
printf("patient age:%d\n", pd1.age);
printf("patient disease: %s\n", pd1.disease);
printf("fee: %f\n", pd1.fee);
return 0;
}
```

Output :

patient id is 1
patient Name: xyz patient age:28
patient disease: covid19
fee: 40000.000000

An Example program to illustrate a structure

```
#include<stdio.h>
#include<string.h>
struct patient_Details
{
int patient_id; //structure member
char patient_Name[20]; //structure member int age;
char disease[20]; float fee;
};
int main()
{
```

```
struct patient_Details pd1; //declaration of structure variable
//reading values into structure members printf("Enter patient id");
//initializing data to structure members
scanf("%d", &pd1.patient_id);
printf("Enter patient Name");
scanf("%s", pd1.patient_Name);
printf("Enter age of the patient");
scanf("%d", &pd1.age);
printf("Enter disease");
scanf("%s", pd1.disease);
printf("Enter Hospital fee");
scanf("%f", &pd1.fee);
//print values in structure members
printf("Display patient id : %d\n", pd1.patient_id);
printf("Display patient Name: %s\n",
pd1.patient_Name);
printf("Display patient age:%d\n", pd1.age);
printf("Display disease: %s\n", pd1.disease);
printf("Display hospital fee: %f\n", pd1.fee);
return 0;
}
```

Output :

Enter patient id 1
Enter patient Name xyz
Enter age of the patient 28
Enter disease covid19
Enter Hospital fee 40000
Display patient id :1
Display patient Name : xyz
Display patient age : 28
Display disease :covid19
Display hospital fee : 40000.000000

Explanation:

In the above program

1. Create a structure definition to store patient_Details.
2. Create structure variable(pd1) for patient_Details.
3. Read patient details into structure members using dot(.) operator.
4. Print patient details from structure members using dot(.) operator.

Structure using Pointers

In order to initialize and access structure members by using pointers, an arrow(->) operator should be used.

Structure Definition

struct<structure_Name>
{ datatype member 1;
datatype member 2;
datatype member n;
.
.
};

Structure Variable Declaration using Pointers :

*struct<structure_Name> *var1, *var2;*

- Here *var1 and *var2 is a pointer variables of type

  struct<structure_Name>.

Initialize Structure Members using Pointer :

- In order to initialize structure members by using pointers, an arrow(->) operator should be used.

  1st Way (Static Initialization) :

- Static initialization means initialize structure members at compile time.

  Syntax:
  var1 ->structure member=value;
  Example:
  pr ->patient_id=1;

- Here var1 is a pointer variable. By using the arrow(->) operator, we can initialize structure members.

2nd Way (Dynamic Initialization) :

Dynamic initialization means initialize structure members at run time.

Syntax :

scanf("format specifier", &pointer structure variable ->structure member);

Example :

scanf("%d", &pr->patient_id);

- Here pr is a pointer structure variable.

By using the arrow(->) operator, we can initialize structure members dynamically.

An example program to illustrate structure using pointers

```
#include<stdio.h> #include<stdio.h> struct patient_Details
{
int patient_id;
char patient_Name[20];
int age;
char disease[20];
float fee;
};
void main()
{
//Declare structure variable struct patient_Details pd1; struct patient_Details
*pr;
//Assign structure to structure pointer pr=&pd1;
//Read data into structure members
printf("Enter patient id:");
scanf("%d", &pr->patient_id);
printf("Enter patient Name:");
scanf("%s", pr->patient_Name);
printf("Enter age:");
scanf("%d", &pr->age);
printf("Enter disease:");
scanf("%s", pr->disease);
printf("Enter Hospital fee:");
scanf("%f", &pr->fee);
//Access values from structure members using pointers
```

```
printf("Patient id is :%d\n", pr->patient_id);
printf("Patient Name is :%s\n", pr->patient_Name);
printf("Patient age is :%d\n", pr->age);
printf("Disease is :%s\n", pr->disease);
printf("Hospital fee is :%f\n", pr->fee);
}
```

Output :

```
Enter patient id:1
Enter patient Name:xyz
Enter age:28
Enter disease: covid19
Enter Hospital fee: 40000
Patient id is:1
Patient Name is:xyz
Patient age is:28 Disease is:covid19
Hospital fee is:40000.000000
```

Explanation :

In the above program

1. Create a structure definition to store patient details.
2. Create structure variables, one is pointer variable (*pr) and another one is normal variable(pd1).
3. Assign starting address of a structure variable pd1 to structure pointer variable (*pr) i.e. pr=&pd1; .
4. Read patient details into Structural members using arrow(->) operator.
5. Print patient details from structure members using an arrow(->) operator.

Array of Structures

Consider a scenario where if you want to store patient details like patient_id, patient_name, patient_age, and diseas,e etc.., Here if we want to store three patient details we need to declare three structure variables and if we want to store hundred patient details we need to declare hundred structure variables and it is not good practice to declare hundred structure variables, then to avoid above flow we can go with array of structures .

- If it is an integer array it stores only numeric values, if it is a floating point array it stores only floating values and if it is astructpatient_Details array it stores data of type structpatient_Details only.
- Array of structures is nothing but a collection of data of the same structure in a continuous memory location.

Structure Definition

Structure definition is nothing but collection of structure member *struct* keyword followed by a structure name.

Syntax:

struct<structure_Name>
[
data type member 1;
data type member 2;
.
.
data type member n;
];

Example :

struct patient_Details
[
int patient_id;
char patient_Name[20]; int age;
char disease[20]; float fee;
];

Structure Variable Declaration using Array

After declaration of structure variable memory allocation should be done for structure definition (collection of structure members).

We have two possibilities to declare a structure variable.

1st way (Declare a Structure Variable using Arrays with Structure Definition) :

Syntax:

struct<structure_Name>
[
data type member 1;

data type member 2;

.

.

data type member n;
}array_Name[size];

Example :

struct patient_Details
{
int patient_id;
char patient_Name[20]; int age;
char disease[20]; float fee;
}pd[5];

After execution of array pd[10] memory allocation should be done for the total structure definition.

Assume memory allocation should be like :

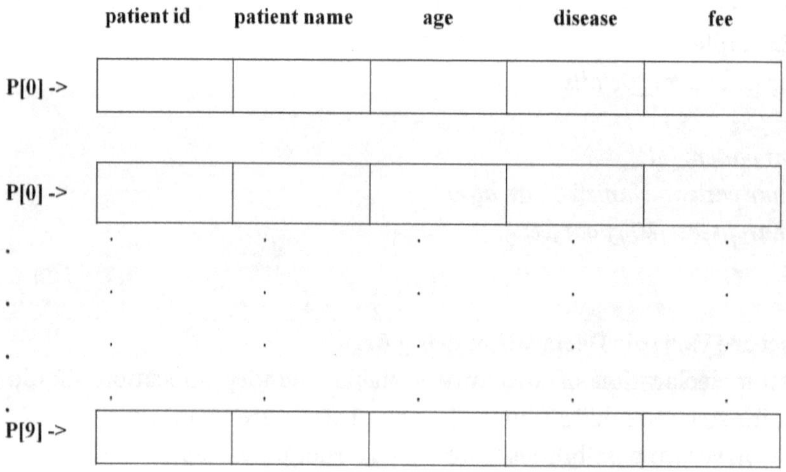

Figure 3.1 Memory allocationof Structure Variables

2nd way (Declare a Structure Variable Using Array Outside the Structure Definition) :

Syntax:

struct<structure_Name>

```
{
datatype member 1;
datatype member 2;
datatype member 3;
.
.
.
datatype member n;
};
void main()
{
struct<structure_Name>array_Name[size];
}
```

Example :

```
struct patient_Details
{
int patient_id;
char patient_Name[20]; int age;
char disease[20]; float fee;
};
void main()
{
struct patient_Details pd[5];
}
```

Above syntax is another way to declare a structure variable in main() function.

Initialize Structure Members By Using Arrays

In order to initialize structure members by using arrays, dot(.) operator should be used i.e. array_Name[index]. Structure Member.

Initialization At Compile Time

Syntax :

```
struct<structure_Name>
array_Name[5];
array_Name[index].structure member=value;
```

Example :

```
struct patient_Details pd[5];
pd[0].patient_id=1;
pd[0].patient_Name="xyz";
pd[0].age=28;
pd[0].disease="covid19";
pd[0].fee=40000;
```

Initialization At Run Time

Syntax :

```
struct<structure_Name>
array_Name[size];
for(int index=0; index<size; index++)
{
scanf("format specifier", &array_Name[index].structure member);
}
```

Example :

```
struct patient_Details pd[5];
for(int p=0;p<5;p++)
{
scanf("%d\t %s\t %d\t %s\t %f", &pd[p].patient_id, pd[p].patient_Name,
&pd[p].age, pd[p].disease, &pd[p].fee);
}
```

After reading data memory allocation should be like :

	patient id	patient name	age	disease	fee
P[0] ->	01	ABC	24	TB	2000
P[0] ->	02	MNO	28	Fever	2500
.	.	.	.	.	.
.	.	.	.	.	.
P[4] ->	05	XYZ	38	Diabetes	4500

Figure 3.2 Data memory allocation

Accessing Structure Members Using Arrays

In order to access structure members using arrays, dot(.) operator should be used.

i.e. array_Name[index].Structure member.

Syntax :

```
struct<structure_Name>array_Name[size];
for(int index=0;index<size;index++)
{
printf("format specifier", array_Name[index].structure Member);
}
```

Example :

```
struct patients_Details pd[5];
for(int p=0;p<5;p++)
{
printf("patient id:%d\n", pd[p].patient_id);
printf("patient Name:%s\n", pd[p].patient_Name);
printf("patient age:%d\n", pd[p].age);
printf("Disease:%s\n", pd[p].disease);
printf("Hospital fee:%d\n", pd[p].fee);
}
```

An example program to illustrate array of structures.

```
#include<stdio.h>
//structure definition struct patient_Details
{
int patient_id;
char patient_Name[20];
int age;
char disease[20];
float fee;
};
void main()
{
//Declare structure variable using arrays struct patient_Details pd[5];
//Initializing structure members using arrays for(int p=0;p<5;p++)
{
printf("Enter patient %d id:", p+1);
scanf("%d", &pd[p].patient_id);
```

```
printf("Enter patient%d Name", p+1);
scanf("%s", &pd[p].patient_Name);
printf("Enter patient %d age", p+1);
scanf("%d", &pd[p].age);
printf("Enter patient %d Disease",p+1);
scanf("%s", &pd[p].disease);
printf("Enter patient %d fee"p+1);
scanf("%d", &pd[p].fee);
}
printf("\n---------------------------- \n");
//Accessing structure members using arrays printf("Details Registered are\n");
for(int p=0;p<5;p++)
{
printf("\npatient %d\t id :%d\n", p+1, pd[p].patient_id);
printf("\npatient %d\t Name :%s\n", p+1, pd[p].patient_Name);
printf("\npatient %d\t age :%d\n", p+1, pd[p].age);
printf("\npatient %d\t disease :%d\n", p+1, pd[p].disease);
printf("\npatient %d\t fee:%d\n", p+1,pd[p].fee);
}
}
```

Output:

```
Enter patient 1 id:1
Enter patient1 Name ravi
Enter patient1 age 28
Enter patient 1 Disease covid19
Enter patient 1 fee 5000
Enter patient 2 id:2
Enter patient2 Name rama
Enter patient2 age 29
Enter patient2 Disease fever
Enter patient2 fee 300
Enter patient 3 id:3
Enter patient3 Name seetha
Enter patient3 age 30
Enter patient3 Disease diabetis
Enter patient3 fee 400
Enter patient 4 id:4
Enter patient4 Name raju
```

```
Enter patient4 age 31
Enter patient4 Disease B.P
Enter patient4 fee 500
Enter patient 5 id:5
Enter patient5 Name ramesh
Enter patient5 age 32
Enter patient5 Disease cough
Enter patient5 fee 600
patient 1 Name :ravi
patient 1 age :28
patient 1 disease :covid19
patient 1 fee :5000.00
patient 2 Name :ramu
patient 2 age :29
patient 2 disease :fever
patient 2 fee :300.00
patient 3 Name :seetha
patient 3 age :30
patient 3 disease :diabetis
patient 3 fee :400.00
patient 4 Name :raju
patient 4 age :31
patient 4 disease :B.P
patient 4 fee :500.00
patient 5 Name :ramesh
patient 5 age :32
patient 5 disease :cold
patient 5 fee :600.00
```

Explanation :

In the above program

1. Create a structure definition to store patient details.
2. Create structure variable, i.e. structpatient_Detailspd[5].
3. Initialize structure members using arrays.
4. Repeat the loop to print values of a structure member until the condition is false.

Nested Structure:

Collection of one or more structures inside another structure is known as Nested Structure.

(Or)

One or more structures under the single structure are known as Nested structure.

Structure Definition

Here we have many possibilities to define nested structure.

Syntax(1st way):

```
struct<outer_structure_Name>
{
datatype member 1;
datatype member 2;
.
.
datatype member n; struct<inner_structure_Name1>
{
datatype member 11;
datatype member 12;
.
.
datatype member 1n;
};
struct<inner_structure_Name2>
{
datatype member 21;
datatype member 22;
.
.
datatype member 2n;
};
};
```

- Here under one structure, i.e. The struct<outer_structure_Name> has 2 inner structures,i.e. struct<inner_structure_Name1> and

```
struct<inner_structure_Name2>
```

Syntax(2nd way) :

```
struct<structure_Name1>
{
datatype member 1;
datatype member 2;
.
.
datatype member n;
};
struct<structure_Name2>
{
```

Syntax(3rd Way) :

```
struct<outer_structure_Name>
{
datatype member 1;
struct<inner_structure_Name>
{
datatype member 2;
struct<inner_most_structure_Name>
{
datatype member 3;
};
};
};
```

Variable Declaration, Initialization and Accessing Structure Members

1st way:

Variable Declaration :

```
struct<outer_structure_Name>outer;
struct<inner_structure_Name 1>inner 1;
struct<inner_structure_Name 1>inner 2;
```

Initialization :

```
outer.member 1=value;
outer.member 2=value;
```

outer.member n=value;
outer.inner1.member 11= value;
outer.inner1.member 12= value;
outer.inner1.member 1n= value;
outer.inner1.inner2.member 21= value;
outer.inner1.inner2.member 22= value;

Accessing :

printf("format specifier", outer.member 1);
printf("format specifier", outer.member 2);
printf("format specifier", outer.inner1.member 11);
printf("format specifier", outer.inner1.member 12);
printf("format specifier", outer.inner1.inner2.member 21);
printf("format specifier", outer.inner1.inner2.member 22);

2nd way :

Variable declaration :

struct<outer_structure_Name>outer;

Initialization :

outer.inner.member 1= value;
outer.inner.member 2= value;
outer.member 11= value;
outer.member 12= value;

Accessing :

printf("format specifier", outer.inner.member 1);
printf("format specifier", outer.inner.member 2);
printf("format specifier", outer.member11);
printf("format specifier", outer.member 12);

3rd way :

Variable Declaration :

struct<outer_structure_Name>outer;
struct<inner_structure_Name>inner;
struct<inner_most_structure_Name>innermost;

Initialization :

outer.member 1= value;
outer.inner.member 2= value;
outer.inner.innermost.member 3= value;

Accessing:

```
printf("format specifier", outer.member 1);
printf("format specifier", outer.inner. member 2);
printf("format specifier", outer.inner.innermost.member 3);
```

Example 1:

An example program to illustrate nested structures (1st way):

```
#include<stdio.h>
#include<string.h>
#include<stdlib.h>
struct patient_Details
{
int patient_id;
char patient_Name[20];
struct hospital_Details
{
char hospital_Name[20];
char doctor_Name[20];
};
struct address
{
char hospital_address[20];
char patient_address[20];
};
float fee;
struct hospital_Details h;
struct address a;
};
void main()
{
struct patient_Details p;
struct hospital_Details h;
struct address a; p.patient_id =1;
strcpy(p.patient_Name, "xyz");
p.fee=4000; strcpy(p.h.hospital_Name, "MXcure");
strcpy(p.h.doctor_Name, "Dr.DP");
strcpy(p.a.hospital_address, "Amalapuram");
strcpy(p.a.patient_address, "udimudi");
//Access structure members
```

```
printf("patient id: %d\n", p.patient_id);
printf("patient Name: %s\n", p.patient_Name);
printf("patient fee: %f\n", p.fee);
printf("Hospital Name: %s\n", p.h.hospital_Name);
printf("Doctor Name: %s\n", p.h.doctor_Name);
printf("Hospital Address: %s\n", p.a.hospital_address);
printf("Patient address: %s\n", p.a.patient_address);
}
```

Output :

```
patient id: 1 patient Name: xyz
patient fee: 4000.000
Hospital Name: MXcure
Doctor Name: Dr.Dp
Hospital Address: Amalapuram
Patient address: udimudi
```

Explanation :

In the above program,

Create nested structure definition structpatient_Details inside patient_Details. Create structhospital_Details and struct address structures.

Read data into structure members using dot(.) operator i.e. p.patient_id=1, p.patient_Name="xyz", etc.

Print data from structure members from nested structure.

Example 2 :

An example program to illustrate nested structures (2nd way)

```
#include<stdio.h>
#include<string.h>
struct patient_Details
{
int patient_id;
char patient_Name[20];
float fee;
char patient_address[20];
};
struct hospital_Details
{
char hospital_Name[20];
char doctor_Name[20];
```

```
char hospital_address[20];
structpatient_Detailspd;
};
void main()
{
struct hospital_Details hd;
hd.pd.patient_id =1;
strcpy(hd.pd.patient_Name, "xyz");
hd.pd.fee =40000;
strcpy(hd.pd.patient_address, "Amalapuram");
strcpy(hd.hospital_Name, "MX cure");
strcpy(hd.doctor_Name, "Dr.DP");
strcpy(hd.hospital_address, "udimudi");
//Access values from nested structure members
printf("Patient id is %d\n", hd.pd.patient_id);
printf("Patient Name is %s\n", hd.pd.patient_Name);
printf("Patient fee is %f\n", hd.pd.fee);
printf("Patient Address is %s\n",hd.pd.patient_address);
printf("Hospital Name is %s\n", hd.hospital_Name);
printf("Doctor Name is %s\n", hd.doctor_Name);
printf("Hospital Address is %s\n",hd.hospital_address);
}
```

Output :

```
Patient id is 1
Patient Name is xyz
Patient fee is 40000.00000
Patient Address is Amalapuram
Hospital Name is MX cure
Doctor Name is Dr.DP
Hospital Address is udimudi
```

Explanation :

In the above program,

1. Create structure definitions structpatient_Details and structhospital_Details and declare structure variable for structpatient_Details inside structure structhospital_Details.
2. Read data into Structural members using dot (.) operator i.e. hd.pd.patient_id=1, hd.pd.patient_Name="xyz". etc..,

3. Print data from structure members from nested structure.

Introduction to Union

- Union is a user defined datatype, which is used to store data with different types, and can access only one value at a time because the memory allocation should be happening based on the largest size of data members.
- Union and structure are of the same flavour, but different in memory allocation.

Similarities between Union and Structure:

- Both are user defined data types.
- Both stores elements with different data types.
- Initializing and accessing data members of both are done by using dot(.) operator.

Differences between Union and Structure:

- The size of the structure is the sum of sizes of all data members (separate member has separate memory).
- Whereas, the size of the union is the size of the largest data member.

Union Definition

Whenever union definition is done, memory allocation will not happen.

- When union variable is declared memory allocation(will happen)is done.

Syntax :

union<union_Name>
[
datatype member 1;
datatype member 2;
.
.

.
datatype member n;
};
Example of Union Definition:-
union patient_Details
{
int patient_id;
char patient_Name[20];
int age;
char disease[20];
float fee;
};

- Here we can use union keyword followed by union name.
- Union name should not be any C keyword and follow the rules of identifier.
- Union members are of mixed type or the same type.
- Union definition should end with semicolon (;).
- Above Union definition contains different types of data types like int, char, and float.
- Memory should not allocate at the time of union definition.

Declaration of Union Variable

Here we have two possibilities to declare Union variable.

1. Declaration of Union variable to Union definition.
2. Declaration of Union variable outside the Union definition.

Whenever a union variable is declared, then only memory is allocated to union members, but not at union definition.

Declaration of Union Variable With Union Definition

Here there is a provision to declare a union variable along with union definition, i.e., declare a union variable next to close bracket (}) of union definition and before the semicolon(;) of union definition.

Syntax:
union <union_Name>
{
datatype member 1;
datatype member 2;
.

```
.
.
datatype member n;
} var1, var2, var n;
```

Example :

```
union patient_Details
{
int patient_id;
char patient_Name[20];
int age;
char disease[20];
float fee;
}pd1, pd2;
```

- Whenever the compiler executes the union variable pd1, pd2 then only memory allocation done for member variables or fields of a union.

Declaration of Union Variable Outside the Union Definition

Here we have another provision to declare a union variable outside the union definition, i.e., declare a union variable inside a main() function.

Syntax:

```
union<union_Name>
{
datatype member 1;
datatype member 2;
.
.
datatype member n;
};
main()
{
union<union_Name>var1, var2;
}
```

Example :

```
union patient_Details
{
int patient_id;
char patient_Name[20];
```

```
int age;
char disease[20];
int fee;
};
void main()
{
union patient_Details pd1, pd2;
}
```

Initialization of Union Members

In order to initialize union members, dot(.) operator should be used.

Union Definition:

```
union patient_Details
{
int patient_id;
char patient_Name[20];
int age;
char disease[20];
float fee;
};
```

1st Way (Initialize at Compile time) :

Syntax:

```
union<union_Name>variable_Name={value 1, value2,........ value n};
```

Example:

```
main()
{
union patient_Details pd1={1, "xyz", 28, "covid19", 40000};
}
```

- Here value 1 stores in patient_id, "xyz" stores in patient_Name, 28 stores in age, "covid19" stores in disease and 40000 stores in fee variables.

2nd Way(Initialize at compile time) :

Syntax :

```
union<union_Name>variable_Name; variable_Name.union member=value;
```

Example :

```
main()
{
union patient_Details pd1;
pd1.patient_id=1;
pd1.patient_Name="xyz";
pd1.age=28;
pd1.disease="covid19";
pd1.fee=40000;
}
```

3rd way (Initialize at run time) :

Syntax:

scanf("format specifier", &union variable.union member);

Example:

```
main()
{
union patient_Details pd1;
printf("Enter patient id");
scanf("%d\n", pd1.patient_id);
printf("Enter patient Name");
scanf("%s\n", pd1.patient_Name);
printf("Enter age");
scanf("%d\n", &pd1.age);
printf("Enter disease");
scanf("%s\n", pd1.disease);
printf("Enter fee");
scanf("%f\n", &fee);
}
```

- Here we can initialize the values at run time by using dot(.) operators, i.e. Union variable, union member.

Accessing Union Members

In order to access union members, dot(.) operator should be used.

Syntax:

union variable.union_member;

An Example program to illustrate a Union

```
#include<stdio.h>
#include<string.h>
union patient_Details
{
int patient_id;
char patient_Name[20];
float fee;
};
int main()
{
union patient_Details pd1;
pd1.patient_id=1;
strcpy(pd1.patient_Name, "xyz");
pd1.fee=500.66;
//Accessing structure members
printf("patient id is %d\n", pd1.patient_id);
printf("patient Name: %s\n",
pd1.patient_Name);
printf("fee: %f\n", pd1.fee);
return 0;
}
```

Output :

```
patient id is 1
patient Name: xyz
fee:500.66
```

Explanation :

In the above program,

- Create Union definition to store patient_Details.
- Create a union variable, i.e. union patient_Details pd, then 20 bytes of memory is allocated.
- Initialize union members using the dot(.) operator.
- Print values of union members usthe ing dot(.) operator.

But here output for patient_id and patient_Name is corrupted and outa put for fee will print as usual without any corruption. Becase, 20 bytes of single memory will allocate and above all 3 union members are pointed to single memory. Firstly patient_id is stored and next patient_Name is stored in the same memory location then the previous value of patient_id is overridden by patient_Name and fee is stored in the same memory location then the previous value of patient _Name is override by fee. Then if you try to access patient_id and Patient_Name it shows corrupted value as shown in above output.

6. TYPEDEF IN C :

The keyword typedef gives permission to alternative names for the primitive example int, float, and derived data types(e.g struct, union)

Use typedef with primitive data type :

The typedef gives an alias name to the existing data type but it does not create a new data type with an alias name.

Syntax :

typedef<Existing_Name><alias_Name>

Example :

typedef int dkint;

Here is the integer data type and dkint is an alias name for int, it works like an int

Use typedef with the derived data type(struct, union)

1. typedef with struct :

There is no need to use the struct keyword again and again in case of using typedef as a prefix to a struct.

Example :

```
#include<stdio.h>
typedef Struct Student
{
int roll;
char name[100];
}std;
main()
{
```

```
std s1,s2;
s1.roll = 48;
cpy(s1.name,"Manasa");
s1.roll = 24;
cpy(s2.name,"Mani Kumar");
printf("%d %s \n",s1.roll,s1.name);
printf("%d %s \n",s2.roll,s2.name);
}
```

Explanation :

In the above program, we use typedef as a prefix to struct student

Without typedef, we need to declare a structure variable like struct student STD, quite big after that in the above program

We simplify it by using the typedef keyword

We need to declare a structure variable like std s1, s2.

Here std is an alias name for struct student.

2. typedef with Union :

There is no need to use the Union keyword again and again in case of using typedef as a prefix to Union.

Example:

```
#include< stdio.h >
#inlcude< string.h >
typedef union student
{
int roll;
char name[20];
}std;
main( )
{
Std s1,s2;
s1.roll = 48;
cpy(s1.name,"Manasa");
s2.roll = 24;
cpy(s1.name,"Koti");
printf("%d 5s \n",s1.roll,s1.name);
printf("%d 5s \n",s2.roll,s2.name);
}
```

Explanation :

In the above program, we use typedef as a prefix to struct student

Without typedef, we need to declare a structure variable like struct student STD, quite big after that in the above program

We simplify it by using the typedef keyword

We need to declare a structure variable like std s1,s2.

Here std is an alias name for struct student.

IV

POINTERS

CONTENTS: Introduction, Pointers to pointers, Pointer Arithmetic, Compatibility, L value, and R value Pointer Applications: Arrays, and Pointers, Memory Allocation Function, Array of Pointers, Strings using pointers, Dangling pointers, Processor Commands: Processor Commands.

1. INTRODUCTION TO POINTERS

A pointer is a container that stores/hold the address of another variable.

> "*According to* ***Mark Burgess*** *(4th edition). "A pointer is a special type of variable which holds the address or location of another variable."(P.77).*"

Here the normal variable holds/stores value in main memory, but while coming to pointer variable it holds/stores address of another variable. The capability of a pointer variable is to store the address of the memory location. Pointer means the name itself says that points to another variable memory location.

Declare Pointer Variable

*datatype *Variable_Name;*

Or

datatype Variable_Name;*

Example:

```
int *pr;//integer pointer
float *pr; //floating pointer
char *pr; //character pointer
double *pr; //double pointer
```

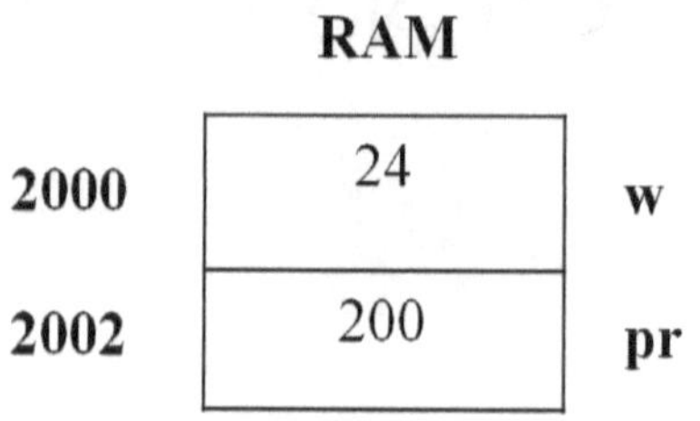

Figure 4.1 Memory Allocation

Initialization of Pointer Variable

int w=24; //variable

int *pr=&w; //pointer variable initialization

Pointer variable initializes by using address of a variable.

Accessing Pointer Variable

int w=24;//variable initialization

*int *pr = &w; //pointer initialization, store address of variable in pr, i.e. 2000*

*printf("%d", *pr);//accessing value*

- Here, the statement int w= 24; after executing it allocates 2 or 4 bytes of memory and "w" is the name given to that memory location and assumes 2000 is the address of that memory location.
- After execution of the statement **int *pr = &w;** then allocates 2 or 4 bytes of memory and "pr" is the name given to that memory location assume 2002 is the address of that memory location and here the pointer variable(pr) holds the address of variable "w", i.e. address of w is 2000.
- The statement printf("%d", *pr); gives 24 as output.

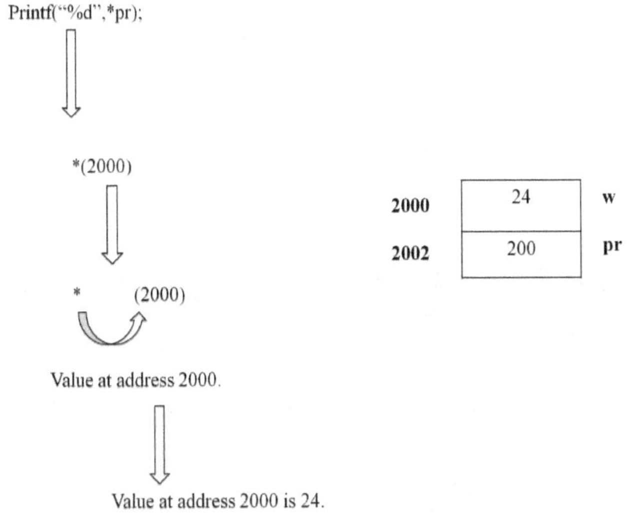

Figure 4.2 Process of execution of the print statement

Example:

An example program to illustrate pointers.

```
#include<stdio.h> void main()
{
int w=24;
int *pr = &w;
printf("Value of w:\n%d\n", w);
printf("Value at pr:\n%u\n", pr);
printf("Address of variable w:\n%u\n", &w);
printf("Address of pointer variable pr:\n%u\n", &pr);
printf("Value at the address:\n%u\n", *pr);
}
```

Memory location:

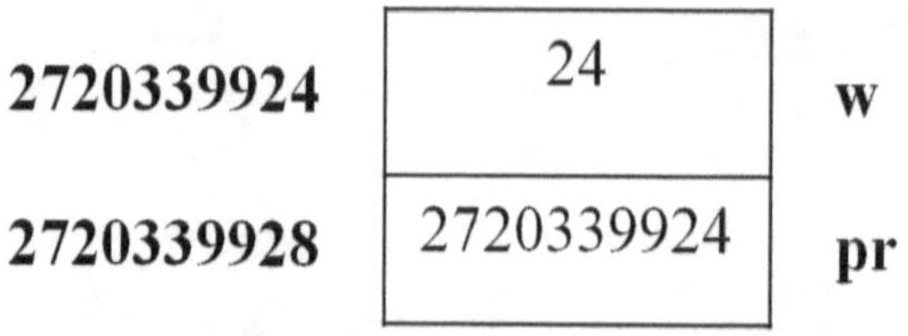

Figure 4.3 Memory Allocation

Output:
Value of w:
24
Value at pr: 2720339
924
Address of variable w: 2720339924
Address of pointer variable pr: 2720339928
Value at the address: 24

Explanation:
In the above program

1. We declare and initialize a variable “w” with 24 and the address location for variable w is 2720339924.
2. In the statement, int *pr = &w, i.e. The pointer variable stores address of variable “w” (2720339924).
3. print(“%u\n”, pr); i.e. It prints the value at pr. Here, the value is nothing but the address of variable “w” (2720339924). The statement prints 2720339924.
4. print(“%u\n”, &w); i.e. Here the address of variable “w” is 2720339924.
5. print("%u\n", &pr);i.e. Here the address of pointer variable “pr” is 2720339928.
6. The statement, printf("%u\n", *pr);it prints 24 because

pr→(value at pr) →*(2720339924). Here the dereferencing operator(*) is present before the address 2720339924 and gives the value at the address i.e. 24.

2. POINTERS TO POINTERS

Pointer to pointer is also known as double pointer. Normally pointer holds the address of a variable and in the same way double pointer holds the address of another pointer.

Syntax:

datatype **ptop;

Example:

```
int w = 24;
int *pr = &w;
int **ptop = &pr;
```

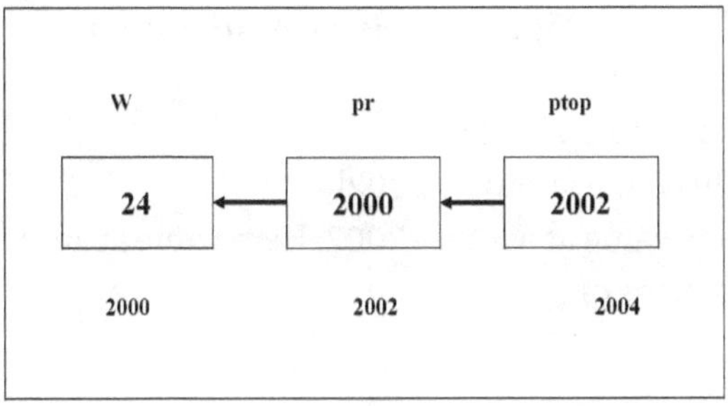

Figure 4.4 Pointer to Pointer

Change the Variable by Using a Double Pointer:

Declare a variable 'w' and initialize with 24 and change the value of variable 'w' by using the double pointer.

Example:

```
#include<stdio.h>
void main()
{
int w=24;
int *pr = &w;
int **ptop = &pr;
**ptop = 29;
printf("Value at variable w: %d", w);
}
```

Output:

Value at variable w: 29

Explanation:

Before changing the value:

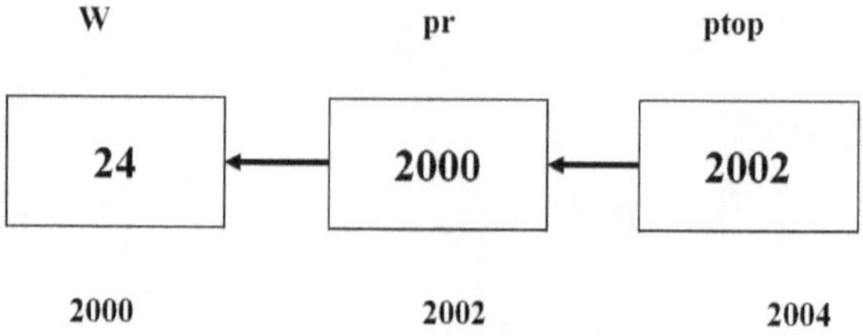

Figure 4.5 Memory allocation

Here **ptop -> *(*(ptop)) = 29

((2002)) = 29 [value at ptop = 2002]

[*(2002) means value at address 2002. Here value at address 2002 is 2000. Replace 2000 in place of

*(2002)]

↓

*(2000)=29

Here *(2000) means the value at address 2000 is replaced with 29.

After changing the value:

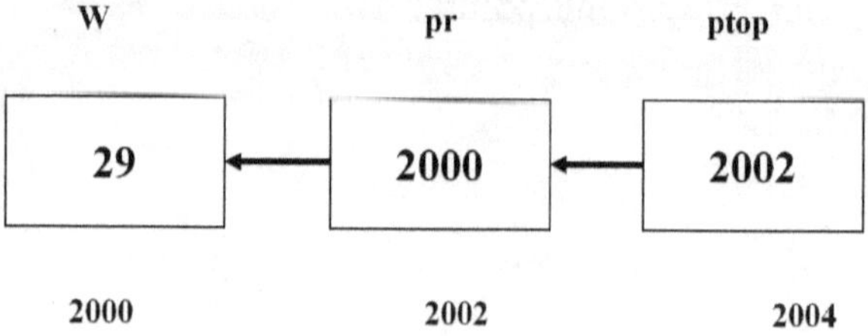

Figure 4.6 Memory allocation

An example program to illustrate double pointer (or) pointer to pointer.

```
#include<stdio.h>
void main()
{
int w = 24;//variable declaration and initialization
int *pr= &w;//assign address of w to pointer pr
int **ptop = &pr; // assign address of pointer pr to double pointer ptop
printf("Value at variable w before change:%d\n", w);
//print value at variable w by using doublepointer
printf("Value at variable w before changing by using double pointer:%d\n",
**ptop);
//changing the value at variable w by using double pointer
**ptop = 29;
printf("Value at variable w after change:%d\n", w);
//print value at variable w by using double pointer
printf("Value at variable w after change: %d\n",**ptop);
}
```

Output:

Value at variable w before the change: 24

Value at variable w before changing by using double pointer: 24

Value at variable w after the change: 29 Value at variable w after the change: 29

3. POINTER ARITHMETIC

Pointers do not support all types of arithmetic operations on pointer variables.

Pointers support mainly arithmetic operations like

1. Increment
2. Pointer decrement
3. Adding constant to a pointer
4. Subtract constant from pointer

Note:

- The addition of two addresses is not possible.
- Multiplication of two addresses is not possible.
- Division and modulus on two addresses are not possible.

Pointer Increment:

It never increments the address value by 1, the incrimination of an address depends upon the size of the pointer data type.

Let me explain with an example,

```
#include<stdio.h>
void main()
[
int w = 24; int *pr= &w;
printf("Address of a pointer holds before increment: %u\n", pr);
pr++; //pointer increment
printf("Address of a pointer holds after increment: %u\n", pr);
]
```

Output:

Address of a pointer holds before increment: 2901362308

Address of pointer holds after increment: 2901362310

Explanation:

Assume memory allocation should be like this and integer size is 2 bytes.

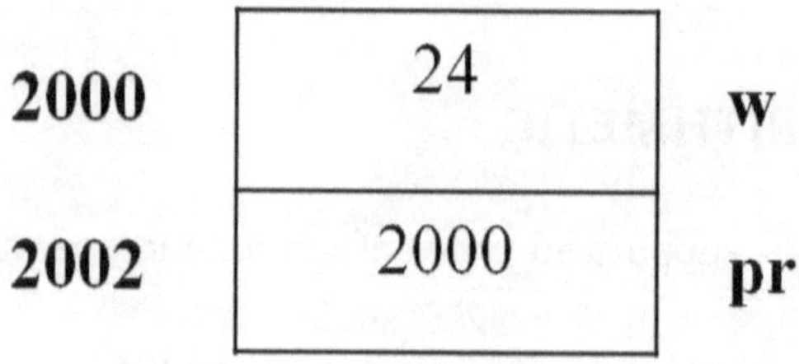

Figure 4.7 Memory Allocation

Generally, we think that pointer increment means incrementing the address by 1, but our assumption is absolutely wrong. Actually incrementing means the pointer points to the next memory location. Here we have the formula to calculate this, i.e.

Pointer_value + (increment_value) * size_of_the_pointer_datatype

Example:

Here, Assume a pointer value is 290136**2308**, the increment value is 1 and the data type of pointer is int i.e. 2 bytes.

If we do pr++ then,
= (2901362**308**) +1*(sizeof (int))
= (2901362**308**) +1*(2)
=2901362**308**+2
=2901362**3010**

After doing pr++ the pointer (pr) points to the next address location 2901362**3010**.

S.N o	Pointer with datatype	Size of the datatype	Value(address)in pointer	Pointer increme nt	After increment value (address)in pointer[pointer _value+ (increment_val u e)*size of pointer datatype
1	int *pr	2 bytes	2000	pr++	2000+1*(2)= 2002
2	Char*pr	1 byte	2000	pr++	2000+1*(1)= 2001
3	Float*pr	4 bytes	2000	pr++	2000+1*(4)= 2004
4	Double*pr	8 bytes	2000	pr++	2000+1*(8)= 2008

Table 4.1 Pointer Increment

Pointer Decrement:

It never decrements the address value by 1, the decrementation of an address depends upon the size of the pointer data type.

Let us take an example:

```
#include<stdio.h>
void main()
{
int w=24;
int *pr =&w;
printf("Address of a pointer holds before decrement: %u\n", pr);
pr--;//pointer decrement
```

printf("Address of a pointer holds after increment: %u\n", pr);
}

Output:

Address of a pointer holds before decrement: 2063695876
Address of a pointer holds after decrement: 2063695874
Explanation:

Actually decrementing means the pointer points to the previous memory location. We have the formula to calculate this, i.e.

(Pointer_value(address)) – (decrement_value) * (size_of_pointer_datatype)

Example :

Here, Pointer value is 206369**5876**, decrement value is 1 and the datatype of pointer is

int =2 bytes(size).
If we do "pr--" then
= (206369**5876**) - 1*(sizeof(int))
= (206369**5876**) - 1*(2)
= (206369**5876**) -2
=206369**5874.**

After doing pr-- the pointer(pr) points to the previous address location 206369**5874**

S.N o	Pointer with datatype	Size of the datatype	Value(address)in pointer	Pointer decreme nt	After increment value (address)in pointer[pointer _ value+ (decrement_va lu e)*size_of _pointer _datatype]
1	int *pr	2 bytes	2000	pr--	2000-1*(2)= 1998
2	Char*pr	1 byte	2000	pr--	2000-1*(1)= 1999
3	Float*pr	4 bytes	2000	pr--	2000-1*(4)= 1996
4	Double*pr	8 bytes	2000	pr--	2000-1*(8)= 1992

Table 4.2 Pointer decrement using different data type

Adding Constant Value to a Pointer:

Here, we can add a constant value or integer value to a pointer but not two pointers.

Syntax for adding a constant value to a pointer:

*[address (or) pointer_value] +[constant_value (or) integer_value] *[size_of_the_pointer_dataype]*

*(Pointer_value(address)) – (decrement_value) * (size_of_pointer_datatype)*

*(Pointer_value(address)) – (decrement_value) * (size_of_pointer_datatype)*

Case 1: Add constant value to an integer pointer:

int w= 24;

int *pr = &w;

Pointer datatype	Size of pointe r datatype	Value (address) in a pointer	Constant value	Add constant value to a pointer(address+co nstant* size of (datatype))
Int	2 bytes	2000	2	2000+2 * 2 =2004
			5	2000+5 * 2 = 2010
			7	2000+7 * 2 = 2014
			10	2000+10 * 2 = 2020

Table 4.3 Add constant value to an integer pointer

Case 2: Add constant value to a character char w = 'd';

char *pr = &w;

Pointer datatype	Size of pointe r datatype	Value (address) in a pointer	Constant value	Add constant value to a pointer(address+constant* size of (datatype))
Char	1 bytes	2000	2	2000+2 * 1 =2002
			5	2000+5 * 1 = 2005
			7	2000+7 * 1 = 2007
			10	2000+10 * 1 = 2010

Table 4.4 Add constant value to a character

Case 3: Add constant value to a floating pointer:
float w = 24.34; float *pr = &w;

Pointer datatype	Size of pointe r datatype	Value (address) in a pointer	Constant value	Add constant value to a pointer(address+constant* size of (datatype))
Float	4 bytes	2000	2	2000+2 * 4 =2008
			5	2000+5 * 4 = 2020
			7	2000+7 * 4 = 2028
			10	2000+10 * 4 = 2040

Table 4.5 Add constant value to a floating pointer

Case 4 : Add constant value to a double pointer
double w = 2.4e + 1;
double *pr = &w;

Pointer datatype	Size of pointe r datatype	Value (address) in a pointer	Constant value	Add constant value to a pointer(address+co nstant* size of (datatype))
			2	2000+2 * 8 =2016
			5	2000+5 * 8 = 2040
Double	8 bytes	2000	7	2000+7 * 8 = 2056
			10	2000+10 * 8 = 2080

Table 4.6 Add constant value to a double pointer

Subtract Constant Value From a Pointer:

Here, we can subtract a constant value or an integer value from a pointer.

The syntax for subtracting a constant value from a pointer:

[address (or) pointer_value] – [constant_value (or) integer_value] * [size_of_the_pointer_dataype]

Case 1: Subtracting Constant Value From an Integer Pointer:

int w= 24;

int *pr = &w;

Pointer datatype	Size of pointe r datatype	Value (address) in a pointer	Constant value	Add constant value to a pointer(address- constant* size of (datatype))
			2	2000 - 2 * 2 = 1996
			5	2000 - 5 * 2 = 1990
Int	2 bytes	2000	7	2000 - 7 * 2 = 1986
			10	2000 - 10 * 2 = 1980

Table 4.7 Subtracting constant value from an integer pointer

Case 2: Subtracting Constant Value From a Character

char w = 'd';

char *pr = &w;

Pointer datatype	Size of pointe r datatype	Value (address) in a pointer	Constant value	Add constant value to a pointer(address-constant* size of (datatype))
			2	2000-2 * 1 =1998
			5	2000-5 * 1 = 1995
Char	1 bytes	2000	7	2000-7 * 1 = 1993
			10	2000-10 * 1 = 1990

Table 4.8 Subtracting constant value from a character

Case 3:Subtracting Constant Value From a Floating Pointer:

float w = 24.34;

float *pr = &w;

Pointer datatype	Size of pointe r datatype	Value (address) in a pointer	Constant value	Add constant value to a pointer(address-constant* size of (datatype))
			2	2000-2 * 4 = 1992
			5	2000-5 * 4 = 1980
Float	4 bytes	2000	7	2000-7 * 4 = 1972
			10	2000-10 * 4 = 1960

Table 4.9 constant value from a floating pointer

Case 4 :Subtracting Constant Value From a Double Pointer
double w = 2.4e + 1;
double *pr= &w;

Pointer datatype	Size of pointe r datatype	Value (address) in a pointer	Constant value	Add constant value to a pointer(address-constant* size of (datatype))
			2	2000-2 * 8 = 1984
			5	2000-5 * 8 = 1960
Double	8 bytes	2000	7	2000-7 * 8 = 1944
			10	2000-10 * 8 = 1980

Table 4.10 constant value from a double pointer

4. COMPATIBILITY

- Converting One data type to another data type is possible in variables, but while coming to pointers converting one pointer data type to another pointer data type is not possible.
- Pointer compatibility is possible by only converting a pointer with one data type (int) to the same data type (int).

Compatibility types are:
1. Pointer size compatibility.
2. Dereference type compatibility.
3. Dereference level compatibility.

1. Pointer Size Compatibility:

• The size of a pointer in a 32-bit system is 4 bytes and in a 64-bit system is 8 bytes.

• In 32 bit system every pointer holds an address with 4 bytes.

Example:1

Int x =24; // variable

Int *p=&x; //pointe

In the above example, the size of the variable 'x' is 2 bytes and the size of the pointer 'p' is one memory location i.e 4 bytes.

Example:2

Float y =24.29; //variable

Float*p=&y; // pointer

In the above example 2 the size of the variable 'y' is 4 bytes and the size of the pointer 'p' is one memory location i.e 4 bytes.

Example:3

Char z= 'd';

Char *p=&z;

In the above example, 3 the size of the variable 'z' is 1 byte and the size of the pointer 'p' is 1 memory location that is 4 bytes.

In a null shell, the size of the pointer is always the same which does not depends on the data type of the pointer.

2. Dereference Type Compatibility:

The dereference or Indirection operator '*' gives the value of a variable that is pointed by a pointer variable.

- The dereference type is the type of variable that the pointer is referencing.
- In, Dereference type compatibility, Compatibility means things are existing together without any issues or any problem.
- If a pointer of type int pointing to a variable of type int (pointer and variable are of the same type) and both pointer and variable are exists together without any problem is called Dereferencing integer type compatibility.

Example 1:

Int x=24; //variable

```
Int *p=&x; //pointer
```

In the above example, both pointer and variable are of the same type (int) so that is a valid assignment.

- If a pointer of type float pointing to a variable of type float(pointer and variable are of the same type) and both pointer and variable are exists together without any problem is called Dereferencing float type compatibility.

Example:2

```
Float y= 24.29; //variable
Float *p=&y; //pointer
```

In the above example, both pointer and variable are of the same type (float)so that is a valid assignment.

- If a pointer of type char pointing to a variable of type char (pointer and variable are of the same type) and both pointer and variable are exists together without any problem is called Dereferencing char type compatibility.

Example:3

```
Char z= 'd';
Char *p=&z;
```

In the above example both pointer and variable are of same type (char) so that is valid assignment.

- If a pointer of type int pointing to a variable of type float (pointer and variable are of not same type)and both pointer and variable are exists together with a problem or an issue saying that assignment from Incompatible pointer type.

Example:

```
Float x=24.29;
Int *p=&x;
```

In the above example, both pointer and variable do not belong to the same data type so there is an invalid assignment so, this is called incompatible pointer type.

We can overcome the above incompatible pointer type problem with typecasting.

Example:

Float x=24.29;

Int *p=(int *) &x;

It converts a float to an int pointer and assigns value to pointer p.

3. Dereference Level Compatibility:

The first level of compatibility:

Assign the address of a variable to a pointer.

Int x =24;

Int *p=& Int x;

The second level of compatibility:

Assign the address of a pointer to a pointer to pointer.

Int x =24; //variable

Int *p=&x; //pointer

Int **q=&p; // pointer to pointer

Third level of compatibility:

Assign the address of double asterisk pointer i.e pointer to pointer to triple asterisk pointer i. e pointer to a pointer to a pointer

Int x =24; //variable

Int *p=&x; //pointer

Int **q=&p; // pointer to pointer

Int***r=&q;

The compiler allows above levels of compatibility

Example:

Int x =24; //variable

Int *p=&x; //pointer

Int **q=&p; // pointer to pointer

Int ***r=&x;

The compiler does not allow the above levels of compatibility saying that initialization of 'int**' from incompatible pointer type ' int*' int**q=&x;

Saying that initialization of 'int ***' from incompatible pointer type 'int *' int ***r=&x;

5. L value and R value:

L value:

L values (locator value) means it is an object that has some memory with the address.

It includes a variable, constant variable, array elements, function calls, and unions.... Etc...

We can also access the address of L values. By using & operator.

Examples on lvalues:

Example-1

int x=24;

In the above expression x is l values because x has address.

int *p1=&x; //valid

Example-2

int y=x+5;

Here y is l values because memory with address is allocated for variable 'y'.

int *p2=&y; //valid assignment

int *p3=&(x+5) //invalid assignment

//error

The above statement (x+5) is not on lvalue we never access the address of (x+5).

R value:

We cannot access the address of a variable called R value.

The r value is an expression, that does not have memory.

Note:

1. An expression that can be on the left-hand side of an equals to (=) operator is known as L value.
2. An expression that can be on the right-hand side of an equal to (=) operators.
3. An expression that has memory location is known as L value.
4. An expression that has no memory location is known as r value.

Examples on R values:

Example-1

int x=24;
Here 24 is r value because 24 has no memory.
int*p1=& (24); //error.

Example-2

int a=x+5;
int *p2=& (x+5); //error.
(x+5) is an r value.

Common Example:

```
#include<stdio.h>
main()
{
int x=24; //x is l value and 24 is r value
int y=(x+5); // y is l value and (x+5) is r value
int *p1=&x; //possible it can access l value
int *p2=&(x+5) //not possible compile error
}
```

6. ARRAYS TO POINTERS

We know that the array variable holds starting address of an array and gives that starting address of an array to a pointer variable. By using pointers we can access array values.

Example programs:

An example program to illustrate arrays using pointers with increment operator.

```
#include<stdio.h>
void main()
{
int p[5] = {24, 29, 48, 2, 13};
int *pr = &p[0];
printf("Values in array are:\n");
for(int s=0;s<5;s++)
{
printf("%d\t", *pr); pr++;
}
}
```

Memory allocation:

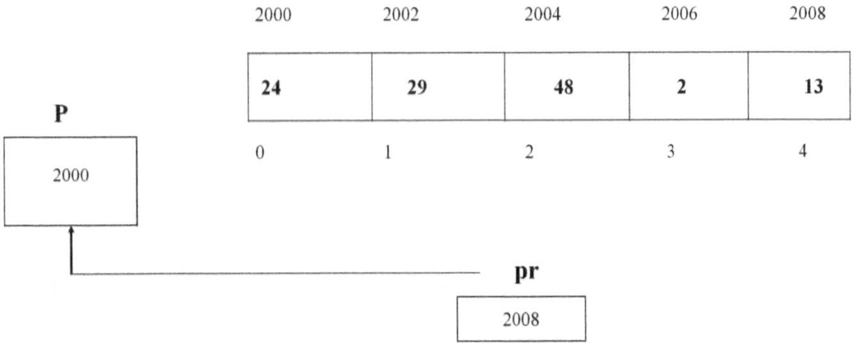

Figure 4.8 Memory allocation

Output:
Values in array are: 24 29 48 2 13
Explanation:
In the above program

1. We declare and initialize a 1-D array.
2. We declare a pointer and initialize it with the starting element address.
3. Repeat the loop to print values in an array by using pointers until the condition becomes false.
4. Here pointer increment(pr++) points to the next memory location.

An example program to illustrate arrays using pointers with decrement operator.

```
#include<stdio.h>
    void main()
    {
    int p[5] = {24, 29, 48, 2, 13};
    int *pr = &p[4];
    printf("Values in array are:\n");
    for(int s=0;s<5;s++)
    {
```

```
printf("%d\t ", *pr);
pr--;
}
}
```

Memory allocation :

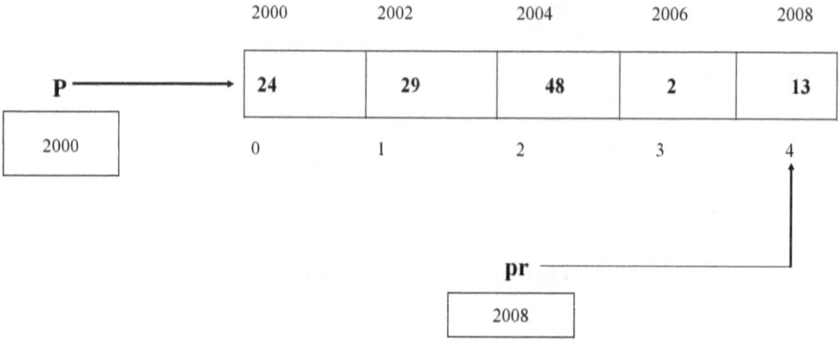

Figure 4.9 Memory allocation

Output:

Values in the array are:

13 2 48 29 24

Explanation:

In the above program

- We declare and initialize a 1-D array.
- We declare a pointer and initialize with p[4].
- Repeat the loop to print values in an array by using pointers until the condition becomes false.
- Here pointer decrement (pr--) points to the previous memory location.

7. STRINGS USING POINTERS

We know that character array variable holds starting address of a 1-D character array and gives the starting address of a 1-D character array to a pointer variable. By using pointers we can access values, character array values/elements.

An example program to illustrate strings using pointers.

```
#include<stdio.h>
void main()
{
char p[13] = "KotiManiKumar";
char *pr = &p[0];
for(int s=0;p[s]!='\0';s++)
{
printf("%c", *pr);
pr++; //pointer increment
}
}
```

Output:

KotiManiKumar

Explanation:

In the above program

- We declare and initialize a 1-D array.
- We declare a character pointer and initialize with the starting address of a character array.
- Repeat the loop to print values/elements in a character array by using pointer and increment the pointer until p[s]!='\0'.

8. DANGLING POINTER

A pointer pointing to a memory location which does not exits is called a dangling pointer.Actually, we know that pointer holds the address of another variable, but after

sometime unknowingly that address location is deleted, but still the pointer points to that memory location which is not present now that pointer is known as dangling pointer.

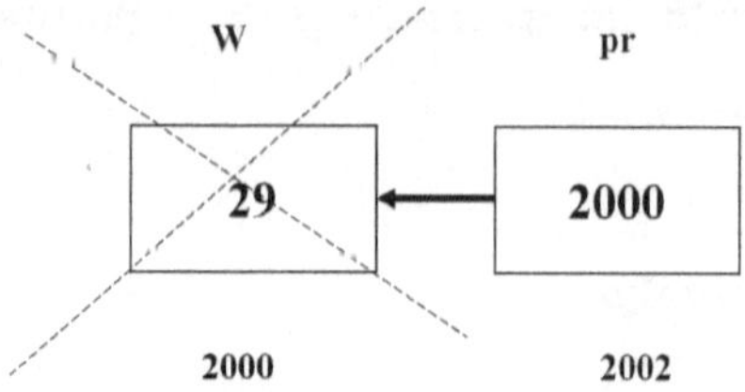

Figure 4.10 Dangling Pointer

Case Study

Case 1:De-allocating/deleting memory using free() function.

```
#include<stdio.h>
void main()
{
int w = 24;
int *pr = &w;
printf("Access variable before deleting: %d", *pr); free(w); //de-allocating memory
printf("Access variable after deleting: %d", *pr);
}
```

Output:

Segmentation fault

Explanation:

- Declare and initialize variable 'w' with 24.
- Declare a pointer variable and assign the address of variable 'w'.
- Print value at variable 'w' by using pointer(*pr) and it prints 24.
- By using free() function, it de-allocates the memory of the variable w, but still pointer pr holds previous address of variable 'w'.
- Print value at variable 'w' by using pointer(*pr) and it shows the result as a segmentation fault.
- Here, the pointer (*pr) is dangling pointer.

Case 2: Illustrate dangling pointer concepts by using functions.

```
#include<stdio.h>
```

```
int dangling_fun();
void main()
{
int *pr = NULL;
pr = dangling_fun();
printf("Address that pointer holds: %u\n", pr);
printf("Print value of a variable by using address: %d", *pr);
}
int dangling_fun()
{
int w=24;
printf("Address of variable w: %u\nValue of variable w: %d\n", &w, w);
return &w;
}
```

Output:

Address of variable w: 2023677516
Value of variable w: 24
Address that pointer holds: 0
Segmentation fault

Explanation:

In the above program

1. We have two functions one is main() and another is dangling_fun().
2. Here, dangling_fun() has a variable 'w' and initialized with 24. Here variable 'w' is local variable to dangling_fun().
3. Next step is to return the address of variable 'w' to the calling function. Whenever the control transfers back to the calling function, then the local variable 'w' memory is de-allocated.
4. In main() function, by using pointer(*pr) if we try to access the variable 'w' value it shows segmentation fault, because variable 'w' is local to the dangling_fun() function after execution of that function completed the memory of variable 'w' is de-allocated.

9. MEMORY ALLOCATION FUNCTION

The main use of **Dynamic Memory Allocation** is to avoid memory wastage. We already know that size of the array is fixed. The array is a static memory allocation. The memory allocation for arrays are done at compile time, it never changes at runtime. In case of dynamic memory allocation, the memory allocation is done at runtime, due to this we can avoid memory wastage.

We can achieve dynamic memory allocation by using 4 functions. All these functions work under stdlib.h header file (or) standard library.

They are:-

- malloc()
- calloc()
- realloc()
- free()

1. *malloc()*

By malloc () function, allocates contiguous block of memory dynamically at run time.

- The default value in allocating memory is garbage value.
- While creating memory dynamically by using malloc () function, On Success, it returns starting address to the pointer.

On failure, it returns **NULL** value of the pointer

Syntax:-

**pr= (cast_type) malloc (size*sizeof (datatype));*

Ex:-

*int *pr = (int*)malloc(5*sizeof(int));*

Here consider the size of the integer is 2 bytes and requested 5*size of(int) memory, i.e., 5*2=10 bytes of memory allocated at runtime for the above statement.

Assume memory allocation for above malloc () function.

An example program to illustrate malloc () function.

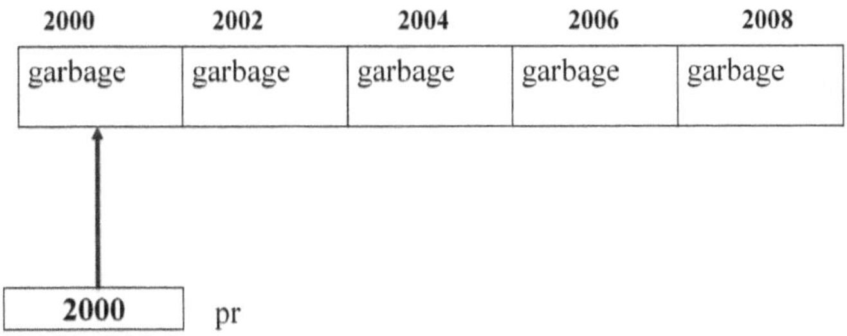

Figure 4.11 Memory Allocation

```
// program
#include<stdio.h>
#include<stdlib.h>
#include<malloc.h>
void main ()
{
int *pr, p, size_arr; printf("Enter size of the array:");
scanf("%d", &size_arr);
pr= (int*)malloc(size_arr*sizeof(int));
if(pr==NULL)
{
printf("Memory not allocated");
exit(0);
}
printf("Enter elements in an array:");
for(p=0;p<size_arr;p++)
{
scanf("%d", &*pr+p);
}
printf("Print elements in an array\n");
for(p=0;p<size_arr;p++)
{
printf("%d\t", *pr);
pr++;
}
}
```

Output:
Enter size of the array:4
Enter elements in an array: 24 29 48 13
Print elements in an array : 24 29 48 13

Explanation:-

In the above program

1. Read the size of an array.
2. Here the size of the array is 4 and malloc () function allocates 4*2=8 bytes of memory (assume the size of the int= 2 bytes) allocates and assume 2000 is the starting address assigned to pointer pr.
3. Check memory allocated or not by using malloc () function returns NULL and control exits from the program.
4. Read the values into an array.
5. Print the values from an array.

Assume memory allocation for the above program should be :

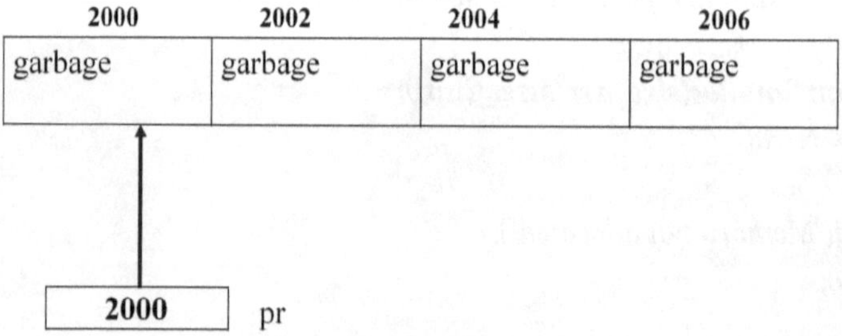

Figure 4.12 Memory Allocation

2. *calloc() Function*

1. It works under stdlib.h or calloc.h header file.
2. Calloc stand for contiguous allocation.
3. Calloc and malloc are same functionality and both are used to allocate block of continuous allocation dynamically at runtime, but the main

difference is the default value of calloc created memory has initialized with zero and the default value of malloc created memory has initialized with garbage value.

4. If there is no problem, while creating memory dynamically by using calloc(), it returns starting address to the pointer otherwise it returns NULL value of the pointer.

Syntax:

*data type *pr= (cast type*) calloc (size, sizeof (data type))*

Example:

*int *pr= (int*) calloc (4, sizeof (int));*

Here consider the size of an integer is 2 bytes and user requested calloc (5, sizeof (int)) memory, i.e. it gives 10 bytes of memory allocated at runtime for the above statement.

Assume memory allocation for the above program should be :

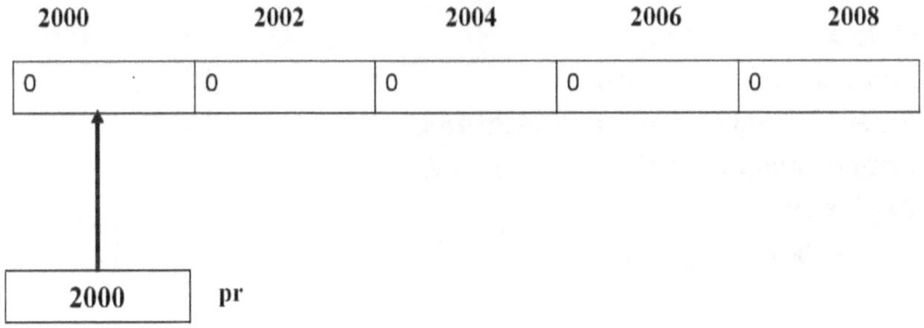

Figure 4.13 Memory allocation for calloc()

An example program to illustrate calloc() function.

```
//program
#include<stdio.h>
#include<stdlib.h>
#include<calloc.h>
void main()
{
int *pr, p, size_arr;
printf("Enter size of the array:");
scanf("%d", &size_arr);
```

```
pr= (int*)calloc(size_arr, sizeof(int));
if(pr==NULL)
{
printf("Memory not allocated"); exit(0);
}
printf("Enter elements in an array:");
for(p=0;p<size_arr;p++)
{
scanf("%d", pr+p);
}
printf("Print elements in an array\n");
for(p=0;p<size_arr;p++)
{
printf("%d\t", *pr);
pr++;
}
}
```

Output:

Enter size of the array: 4

Enter elements in an array: 24 29 48 13

Print elements in an array 24 29 48 13

Explanation:-

In the above program

1. Read the size of an array.
2. Here the size of the array is 4 and calloc () function allocates 4*2=8 bytes of memory (assume the size of the int= 2 bytes) allocates and assume 2000 is the starting address assigned to pointer pr.
3. Check memory allocated or not by using calloc () function returns NULL and control exits from the program.
4. Read the values into an array.
5. Print the values from an array.

3. realloc() Function

1. It works under stdlib.h header file.

2. The **realloc** stands for reallocation of memory.
3. **realloc ()** function resizes the memory which is previously created by malloc() function and calloc() function only.
4. By using **realloc ()** function, we can increase or decrease the memory allocated by malloc() and calloc() functions.

6. It is impossible to resize the memory allocated at compile time (*like variables and arrays*).
7. If we use the **realloc()** function to extend the memory previously allocated by malloc() or calloc() function, **realloc()** function checks 2 points before resizing previous memory.
8. If requested memory is available in that block, the **realloc ()** function simply extends the memory without disturbing the values in previous memory location.
9. If requested memory is unavailable in that block, the realloc () function creates memory in another block and copies the values from a previous memory location in the previous location to newly allocated memory.

Syntax:

*data type *pr =realloc(pr, n*size of(data type))*

Here pr is pointer n is size

An example program to illustrate realloc() function.

//program

```
#include<stdio.h>
#include<stdlib.h>
void main()
{
int *pr, p, size_arr=3, new_size;
pr=(int*)malloc(size_arr*sizeof(int));
if(pr==NULL)
{
printf("Memory not allocated");
exit(0);
}
*(pr+0)=24, *(pr+1)=29, *(pr+2)=48;
printf("Enter new size:");
scanf("%d", &new_size);
pr=realloc(pr, new_size*sizeof(int));
```

```
if(pr==NULL)
{
printf("Memory not allocated");
exit(0);
}
*(pr+3)=13, *(pr+4)=2;
for(p=0;p<new_size;p++)
{
printf("%d\t", *(pr+p));
}
free(pr);
}
```

Output:

Enter new size : 5

24 29 48 13 2

Explanation:

In the above program,

1. Firstly allocates 6 bytes of memory using malloc () function and starting address (say zero) return to a pointer (pr).
2. Initialize

2.1. *(pr+0) =24*(2000+0*2) =>24 =>*(2000) =24
i.e. 24 stores in address 2000.

2.2. *(pr+1) =29 *(2000+1*2) =29 *(2002) =29, i.e.
stores value at address 2002 is 29.

2.3. *(pr+2) =48 *(2002+2*2) =48 *(2004), i.e.
stores value at 2004 is 48.

3. Enter new size, i.e. 5, realloc () function allocates 10 bytes of memory without disturbing previous values. Out of 10 bytes, 6 bytes are filled with values previously and the remaining 4 bytes are filled with new values, i.e.

3.1 *(pr+3) =13 *(2000+3*2)=13 *(2006)=13 i.e.
Stores value at address 2006 is 13.

3.2. *(pr+4) =2 *(2000+4*2) =2 *(2008) =13, i.e.
stores value at address 2008 is 2.

4. Print all the values.

5. Reallocate memory for the pointer pr by using free () function.

4. *free () Function*

It is good practice to free to memory after usage.

For example, if you create a dynamic memory by using malloc() and calloc() functions and after creation, use that memory to store your data/ values and after you done with your work return the memory back to heap by using free() function. The complier uses that memory for another use. The free() function deallocates the memory created by malloc() and calloc() functions.

An example program to illustrate free() function.

//Program

```
#include<stdio.h>
#include<stdlib.h>
void main()
{
int *pr1, *pr2, p;
pr1 =(int*)malloc(3*sizeof(int));
pr2 =(int*)calloc(3, sizeof(int));
*(pr1+0)=24, *(pr1+1)=29, *(pr1+2)=48;
*(pr2+0)=13, *(pr2+1)=2;*(pr2+2)=14;
for(p=0;p<3;p++)
{
printf("Malloc values:%d\ncalloc values:%d\n", *(pr1+p),*(pr2+p));
}
//deallocate memory for pr1&pr2. free(pr1);
free(pr2);
}
```

Output:

Malloc values :29

calloc values :2

Malloc values :48

calloc values :14

Explanation:

In the above program

- Create 6 bytes of memory using malloc() function.
- Create 6 bytes of memory using calloc() function.
- Read data into the memories created by malloc() and calloc() functions.

- After printing data, deallocate memory created by using malloc() and calloc() function and by using free() function.

V

FUNCTIONS AND FILES

CONTENTS: Function in C, Actual and formal parameters, Types of functions, Call by value and Call by reference, Inter-Function Communication, Standard Functions, Passing Array to Functions, Passing Pointers to Functions, Passing Structure to a Function, Recursion

Text Input / Output: Files, Streams, Standard Library Input / Output Functions, Formatting Input / Output Functions, Character Input / Output Functions Binary Input / Output: Text versus Binary Streams, Standard Library Functions for Files.

1. FUNCTION IN C :

A function is a group of statements, that perform a particular task by taking input and giving output.

The main purpose of the functions is code reusability,

i.e. if we want to use the same block of code many times it is good practice to use functions, otherwise lines of code increase then system performance goes down.

It is better to keep the same block of code in a function, whenever you want a code, just call that function by using the function name. Another purpose of the functions is to divide a large program (task) into small blocks (functions) and see there are no dependencies among blocks (functions), due to this it is easy to understand and easy to maintain by other developers and readability will increase.

Note:

Whenever a function is called, separate memory is allocated for each and every function call.

1. Function Declaration (or) Prototype

Whenever the compiler executes the function declaration part which is present above the main() function, then the compiler will come to know the declared function name, function data type and it's the parameter list. Whenever the compiler executes a **calling function** and **function definition,** the compiler compares whether the function name, the data type of the function, and the parameter list are the same or not with a function declaration. If it is the same the compiler executes smoothly without errors, otherwise, it shows an error.

Syntax of Function Declaration

data_type function_Name(<Parameter list>);

2.Function Call (or) Calling Function

By using function call we can call the function/calling function/function definition anywhere in the program.

Syntax: *function_Name(<Parameter list>);* **Example:**

patient_Details(patient_id, patient_Name, fee);

Here, after executing the above **calling function,** the compiler jumps to function name with patient_Details and parameters patient_id, patient_Name, and fee, and its data type and order of parameters must be the same, only then the compiler goes to function definition.

3. Function Definition (or) Called Function

Here function definition contains blocks of statements that need to execute, which takes input from parameters and returns a single value as a result if it is a non-void data type.

Syntax:

data_type function_Name(<parameter list>)

{

//block of statements

}

Example:

```
#include<stdio.h>
int patient_Details(int, float);
int main()
{
int patient_id=48;
float fee=40000.00;
patient_Details(patient_id, fee);
return 0;
}
//function declaration (or) called function int patient_Details(int patient_id, float fee)
{
printf("patient id is %d\n", patient_id);
printf("fee %f\n", fee);
return 0;
}
```

Output:
patient id is 48
fee 40000.000000

2. ACTUAL AND FORMAL PARAMETERS

```
//function declaration (or) prototype data_type function_Name(<Parameter list>) int main()
{
---
// calling function function_Name(<Parameter list>); return 0;
}
//function definition (or) called function data_type function_Name(<Parameter list>)
{
//Function body
}
```

Example:

```
#include<stdio.h>
int patient_details(int id, char Name[20], float fee);
int main()
```

```
{
int patient_id=48;
char patient_Name[20] = "xyz";
float fee=40000.00;
patient_details(patient_id, patient_Name,fee);
return 0;
}
int patient_id=48;
char patient_Name[20] = "xyz";float fee=40000.00;
patient_details(patient_id, patient_Name, return 0;
//function declaration (or) called function
int patient_details(int id, char Name[20], float fee)
{
printf("patient id is %d\n", id);
printf("patient name is %s \n", Name);
printf("hospital fee %f\n", fee);
return 0;
}
```

Output:

patient id is 48
patient name is xyz
hospital fee 40000.00

Actual Parameters:

The parameters which are present at the **calling function** are known as actual parameters.

In the above program the parameters patient_id, patient_Name, and fee are the actual parameters and here patient_id holds 48, patient_Name holds "xyz" and fee holds 40000.

Formal Parameters:

The parameter which is present at the **function definition** or **called function** is known as formal parameters.

In the above program the parameters *id, Name [20], and fee* are the formal parameters.

3. TYPES OF FUNCTIONS

Here we have 4 types of user-defined functions:

- No Arguments and No Return Value.
- No Arguments and Return Value.
- Arguments and Return Value.
- Arguments and No Return Value

No Arguments and No Return Value

Here no arguments mean avoiding placing parameters/arguments in the function definition. No return value means **called function/function definition** does not return a value to the calling function.

If the function data type is void, the function does not expect any return value.

If the function data type is non-void, then the function expects a return value.

Syntax:

```
void fun_Name(); main()
{
fun_Name();
}
void fun_Name()
{
//Statements
}
```

Example program to illustrate No arguments and No return values :

Program:

```
#include<stdio.h>
void fun_add(); //function declaration (or) prototype void main()
{
fun_add(); //calling function
}
void fun_add() //called function (or) funnction definition
{
int p, s, add_val; printf("Enter 1st value:");
```

scanf("%d", &p); printf("Enter 2nd value:");
scanf("%d", &s); add_val=p+s;
printf("sum is : %d", add_val);
}

Output:

Enter 1st value:9
Enter 2nd value:6
sum is : 15

Explanation:

In the above program

- Declared a function with the void data type, the function name is fun_add and without any parameters, i.e. void fun_add (); here function return type is void due to this the function never expects any return value.
- In the main() function, we have a **calling function**, i.e. fun_add(); whenever the calling function is executed the control jumps to **function definition or called function.**
- In **function definition or called function** reads the P value and S value and stores the sum of p and s values in another variable add_val. Print value in add_val and if we try to return value in add_val to **calling function** the compiler throws a warning.
- After completion of execution in the function definition or called function the control returns to the calling function.

No Arguments and Return Value

No argument means avoiding placing parameters or arguments in the function definition and return value means **function definition / called function** returns a value to the **calling function.** If we want to return a value it is possible only whenever the data type of **function definition** is non-void.

Syntax:

return_type fun_Name(); main()
{
fun_Name();
}
return_type fun_Name()

```
{
//statement;
return value;
}
```

Note:

Here return_type means int, float, double, long int, long double etc.

Example program to illustrate No argument and return value

Program:

```
#include<stdio.h>
int fun_add();
void main()
{
int ret_val=fun_add();
printf("Addition of two numbers is:%d", ret_val);
}
int fun_add()
{
int p, s, add_val;
p=24, s=29;
add_val=p+s;
return add_val;
}
```

Output:

Addition of two numbers is:53

Explanation:

In the above program

1. Declared a function with the int data type, the function name is fun_add and without any parameters, i.e. int fun_add (); here function return_type is **int** due to this the function may expect a return value.
2. In main() function, we have a **calling function**, i.e. fun_add() whenever **calling function** is executed the control jumps to **function definition (or) called function.**
3. In **function definition or called function**, reads p and s values and stores the sum of p and s values in another variable add_val and return add_val to **calling function** and store that value in variable ret_val and print the value in variable ret_val.

Arguments and Return Value

The Argument is meant placing parameters or arguments in the **function definition** and the return value means the data type of **function definition / called function** is non-void then the function is eligible to return a value to the **calling function.**

A function with arguments and it is of type non-void then it is called, the arguments with a return value.

Syntax:

```
return_type fun_Name(<Parameter list>);
main()
{
fun_Name(<Parameter list>);
}
return_type fun_Name(<Parameter list>)
{
//statements;
return value;
}
```

An example program to illustrate arguments and return values:

Program:

```
#include<stdio.h>
int fun_add(int, int); //function declaration or prototype
void main()
{
int p, s, ret_val;
p=24, s=29;
ret_val=fun_add(p, s);//calling function
printf("Addition of two numbers is:%d", ret_val);
}
int fun_add(int q, int k)//called function/function definition
{
return q+k;
}
```

Output:

Addition of two numbers is:53

Explanation:

In the above program

1. Declared a function with the int data type, the function name is fun_add, and with parameters, i.e. int fun_add(int, int);
2. In main() function, read values into variables p and s and have calling function, i.e. fun_add(p, s); . Whenever the **calling function** is executed the control jump to **function definition or called function** and copies the values in **calling function** parameters, i.e. actual parameters to the parameters in the **called function,** i.e. formal parameter.
3. Return the value after the addition of value in q and value ink to the calling function and print ret_val on the screen.

Arguments and No Return Value

Arguments means placing parameters or arguments in **the function definition** and *No Return Value* means **function definition / called function** does not return a value to **the calling function.**

A function with arguments and it is of type void then it is called **Arguments and No Return Value.**

Syntax:

```
void fun_Name(<arguments_list>);
void main()
{
fun_Name(<arguments_list>);
}
void fun_Name(<arguments_list>)
{
//statements;
}
```

An example program to illustrate arguments and no return value:

```
#include<stdio.h>
void fun_add(int, int);
void main()
{
int p, s;
```

```
p=24, s=29;
fun_add(p, s);
}
void fun_add(int q, int k)
{
int add_val=q+k;
printf("Addition of two numbers is:%d", add_val);
}
```

Output:

Addition of two numbers is:53

Explanation:

In the above program

1. Declared a function with the void data type, the function name is fun_add and with parameters, i.e. void fun_add(int, int);.
2. In main() function, read values into variable p and variable s and have **calling function**, i.e. fun_add(p, s); whenever the **calling function** is executed the control jumps to **function definition or called function** and copies the values in **calling function** parameters, i.e. actual parameters to the parameters in **called function**, i.e. formal parameters, i.e. value in actual parameter p copies to formal parameter q and value in actual parameter s copies to formal parameter k.
3. Add value in q and value in k and store the result in the add_val variable and print in add_val.

4. CALL BY VALUE AND CALL BY REFERENCE

Here we have two possibilities to pass data to functions

1. Call by value
2. Call by reference

Call by Value:

- Call by value means passing values as parameters from the **calling function** to the called function.
- Here passing values means nothing but copies data actual parameters to formal parameters, i.e. separate memory should allocate for actual and formal parameters.
- Here if you can change the value in the formal parameter after copying from the actual parameter, it cannot reflect on values in actual parameters, because there is a separate memory allocated for actual and formal parameters.

An example program to illustrate call by value:

```
#include<stdio.h>
void change_fun(int);
void main()
{
int p=24;
change_fun(p);
printf("After modify p value at main() function is : %d", p);
}
void change_fun(int p)
{
printf("Before modify p value is : %d\n", p);
p=29;
printf("After modify p value at called function is : %d\n", p);
}
```

Output:
Before modify p value is: 24
After modify p value at called function is : 29
After modify p value at main() function is : 24

Explanation:
In the above program

1. Declare a function with the void data type, function Name is change_fun and with parameter, i.e. void change_fun(int).
2. In main() function, read p value with 24 and having **calling function**, i.e. change_fun(p); Whenever the calling function is executed the control jumps to **function definition or called function** and copies the value in **calling function** parameter i.e. 24 to parameter in the called function.

3. In **function definition /called function,** prints output "Before modifying p value is 24" and after this next statement executes and p value becomes 29 and executes the next statement and prints "After modifying p value at called function is 29".
4. After this statement control goes to the **calling function** and executes the next statement and prints "After modifying p value at main() function is: 24".

In the above program, we have two variables with the same name p. Assume variable p in main() function allocates 2/4 bytes of memory with address 2000 (say) and the variable p is called function allocates 2/4 bytes of memory with address 2008 (say). If you want to change the value of p at address 2008 it never reflects the value of p at memory address 2000.

Call by Reference

- Call by reference means passing the address of a variable as a parameter from the **calling function** to called function.
- Here if we send the address of a variable as a parameter from the calling function. At function definition, declare a pointer to receive addresses from the calling function.
- Here if we want to change the value of a variable that is present at the main() function from **called function** is possible with pointers.

An example program to illustrate call by reference:

```
#include<stdio.h>
void change_fun(int*);
void main()
{
int p=24;
change_fun(&p);
printf("After modify p value at main() function is : %d", p);
}
void change_fun(int *pr)
{
printf("Before modify p value is : %d\n", *pr);
*pr=29;
```

```
printf("After modify p value at called function is : %d\n", *pr);
}
```

Output:

Before modify p value is: 24

After modify p value at called function is : 29

After modify p value at main() function is : 29

Explanation:

In the above program

1. Declare a function with the void data type, function name is change_fun and with parameter, i.e. void change_fun(int*).
2. In the main() function, read p value to 24 and have a **calling function**, with a parameter address of p, i.e. change_fun(&p); Whenever the calling function is executed the control jumps to **function definition or called function** and pass the address of p value to function definition with a pointer parameter to hold address coming from **calling function.**
3. In called function, executes the print statement that prints "Before modify P value is: 24".
4. After executing the next statement p value is changed to 29 by using the address of p.
5. After executing the next statement, the print statement that prints "After modify p value at called function is: 29".
6. After execution of **function definition,** the control goes to **calling function** and a print statement that prints "After modify p value at main() function is: 29".

5. PASSING ARRAYS TO A FUNCTION

Here we should pass an array from calling function to called function/ function definition.

We mainly have three ways to pass arrays:

1. Array with blank subscript / unsized array.
2. Array with size subscript / sized array.
3. Using pointer.

1. Array with Blank Subscript / Unsized Array:

Here declare an array with blank/empty subscript and initialize the values and pass the array name and size of the array to **function definition or called function.**

An example program to illustrate passing unsized array to function:

```
#include<stdio.h>
void fun_arr(int p[], int size_value);
void main()
{
int p[]={24, 48, 29, 13};
int size_value= sizeof(p)/sizeof(int);
fun_arr(p, size_value);
}
void fun_arr(int p[], int size_value)
{
int sum_val=0, k=0;
for( ;k<size_value;k++)
{
sum_val=sum_val+p[k];
}
printf("Sum of array values is : %d", sum_val);
}
```

Output:

Sum of array values is: 114

Explanation:

In the above program

1. Declare a function with the void data type, the function name is fun_arr and with two parameters one is array without size another one is, size of the array, i.e. void fun_arr(int p[], int size_value).
2. In the main() function, initialize the unsized array and calculate the size of the array and the value in the size_value variable and have **calling function** i.e. fun_arr(p, size_value);
3. Whenever the **calling function** is executed the control jumps to **function definition or called function** and copies the elements in an array and the size of the array, i.e. those parameters are known as actual parameter values copied to formal parameters at called function.
4. Repeat for loop to find the sum of the elements in an array until k<size_value.

5. Print the sum value sum_val on the screen and control goes to the calling function.

2. Array with Size Subscript / Sized Array

Here we should declare arrays with a size and initialize the values of an array and pass that array to **called function or function definition.**

An example program to illustrate the passing sized array of functions:

```
#include<stdio.h>
void fun_arr(int p[4], int size_value);
void main()
{
int p[4]={24, 48, 29, 13};
int size_value=((sizeof(p))/(sizeof(int)));
fun_arr(p, size_value);
}
void fun_arr(int p[4], int size_value)
{
int sum_val=0, k;
for(k=0;k<size_value;k++)
{
sum_val=sum_val+p[k];
}
printf("Sum of array values is : %d", sum_val);
}
```

Output:

The Sum of array values is :114

Explanation:

In the above program

1. Declare a function with the void data type, the function name is fun_arr and with two parameters one is array with size another one is, size of the array, i.e. void fun_arr(int p[4], int size_value).
2. In the main() function, initialize the sized array and calculate the size of the array and the value in the size_value variable and have a **calling function** i.e. fun_arr(p, size_value);

3. Whenever the **calling function** is executed the control jumps to **function definition or called function** and copies the elements in an array and the size of the array, i.e. those parameters are known as actual parameter values copied to formal parameters at called function.
4. Repeat for loop to find the sum of the elements in an array until k<size_value.
5. Print the sum value sum_val on the screen and control goes to the calling function.

6. PASSING ARRAY ADDRESS USING POINTERS

Here we should declare an array and initialize the values of an array and pass the address of that array from the **calling function to called function/ function definition.**

An example program to illustrate passing array address using pointer

```
#include<stdio.h>
void fun_arr(int *p, int size_val);
void main()
{
int *p;
int arr_val[4]={24, 48, 29, 13};
int size_val=sizeof(arr_val)/sizeof(int);
p=&arr_val[0];
fun_arr(p, size_val);
}
void fun_arr(int *p, int size_val)
{
int sum_val=0, k;
for(k=0;k<size_val;k++)
{
sum_val=sum_val+*(p+k);
}
printf("Sum of array value is : %d", sum_val);
}
```

Output:

SThe um of array value is: 114

Explanation:
In the above program

1. Declare a function with the void data type, the function name is fun_arr and with two parameters one is a pointer to hold the address of the array another one is the size of the array i.e. void fun_arr(int *p, int size_val).
2. In the main() function, declare an array and initialize the array with elements and declare a pointer p, and assign array address to a pointer, i.e. p=&arr_cal[0]; and having **ca alling function**, i.e. fun_arr(p, size_val) whenever the **calling function** is executed the control jumps to **called function or function definition** and formal parameters holds the address of array and size of the array passed by calling function.
3. Repeat the for loop to find the sum of elements in an array using pointer variables until the condition is false.
4. Print the sum value sum_val on the screen and control goes to the calling function.

7. PASSING STRUCTURE TO A FUNCTION

Here we have two ways to pass a structure to a function as a parameter.

1. Passing structure to a function as a value.
2. Passing structure to a function as a reference.

1. Passing Structure to a Function as a Value

We know that structure is a collection of different data types in a single unit. Here we have a provision to pass a total structure to a function as shown in the below example.

An example program to illustrate passing structure to a function as a value:

```
#include<stdio.h>
#include<string.h>
struct patient_details
{
```

```
int patient_id;
char patient name[40];
float fee;
};
void struct_fun(struct patient_details);
void main()
{
struct patient_details pd;
pd.patient_id=48;
strcpy(pd.patient_name, "xyz");
pd.fee=4000.00;
struct_fun(pd);
}
void struct_fun(struct patient_details pd1)
{
printf("patient id is %d\n", pd1.patient_id);
printf("patient name is %s\n", pd1.patient_name);
printf("hospital fee is %f\n", pd1.fee);
}
```

Output:

patient id is 48
patient name is xyz
hospital fee is 4000.000000

Explanation:

In the above program

1. Define a structure, i.e. structpatient_details with structure members, i.e. int patient_id, char patient_name[40], and float fee.
2. Declare a function, i.e. void struct_fun(struct patient_details Pd1).
3. In main() function, declare a structure variable, i.e. struct patient_details pd. Here pd is a variable of type structpatient_details and reads the data into structure members using dot (.) operator and having a calling function, i.e. struct_fun(pd).
4. Whenever the **calling function** is executed the control jumps to called function or function definition and copies the data in the actual parameter (pd) to the formal parameter (pd1) in the **function definition / called function.**

5. After that in **function definition** access, the data in structure members by using dot (.) operator and after accessing the control goes to the calling function.

2. Passing Structure to a Function as a Reference

Here we can pass the address of a structure variable to a function. If we pass the address of a structure variable in the **calling function** and there should be a structure variable pointer in the **called function/function definition** because the pointer variable can only hold an address.

An example program to illustrate passing structure to a function as a reference

```
#include<stdio.h>
#include<stdio.h>
struct patient_details
{
int patient_id;
char patient_name[40];
float fee;
};
void struct_fun(struct patient_details *pd);
void main()
{
struct patient_details pd;
pd.patient_id=48;
strcpy(pd.patient_name, "xyz");
pd.fee=4000.00;
struct_fun(&pd);
}
void struct_fun(struct patient_details *pd)
{
printf("patient id is : %d\n", pd->patient_id);
printf("patient name is : %s\n", pd->patient_name);
printf("hospital fee is : %f\n", pd->fee);
}
```

Output:

patient id is: 48

patient name is xyz
hospital fee is: 4000.000000
Explanation:
In the above program

1. Define a structure, i.e. struct patient_details with struct members, i.e. int patient_id, char patient_name[40], and float fee.
2. Declare a function with pointer structure variable, i.e. void struct_fun(struct patient_details *pd).
3. In main() function, declare a structure variable, i.e. struct patient_details pd. Here pd is a variable of type struct patient_details and read data into structure members using dot (.) operator and having a **calling function**, i.e. struct_fun(&pd). Here we are passing the address of a structure and receiving function should have a pointer variable of type structpatient_details.
4. Whenever the **calling function** is executed the control jumps to **called function/function declaration** and the address of the structure is passed to the structure variable pointer in the called function.
5. Access the values in structure members by using the arrow (->) operator and control goes to the **calling function.**

8. INTER-COMMUNICATION FUNCTION

Inter-function communication means communication between function and calling function

Whenever the calling function executes the control jumps to called function and executes the function definition and again the calling function. The process of exchanging information between called and calling functions is known as inter-function communication.

There are three types of inter function communications are there
1. Downward communication
2. Upward communication
3. Bidirectional communication

1. Downward communication :

*Arguments without return value are called downward communication

*In this type, the data (parameters) send from the calling function to called function, and then the function (or) function definition receives the data and does the process, and again control returns to the calling function without any data(return value)

Example of downward communication

```
#include<stdio.h>
Void add(int x,int y);
main( )
{
Int x= 24,y=29;
add(x,y);//calling function
}
Void add (int x ,int y)//called (or) function definition
{
printf("Addition is %d ",x+y);
}
```

2. *Upward communication :*

*No argument with return value is called upward communication

*In this type, the data (parameters) do not send from the calling function to called function, and then called function or function definition does the process and again control returns to the calling function with data(return value)

Example for upward Communication

```
#include<stdio.h>
int add( );
main( )
{
int sum =add( );//Calling Function
printf("Addition is %d ",sum);
}
int add( )//Called (Or) Function definition
{
int x = 24,y=29;
return x+y;
}
```

3. Bidirectional communication :

*Arguments with return value are called bidirectional communication

*In this type, the data (parameters) are sent from the calling function to called function, and then called function or function definition receives the data parameters and does the process, and again controls the return to the calling function with data(return value)

Example of Bidirectional communication

```
#include<stdio.h>
int add(int x,int y);
main( )
{
int x= 24,y = 29;
int sum = add(x,y );//calling function
printf("Addition is %d",sum);
}
int add(int x,int y)//Called function (or) Functiion definition
{
return x+y;
}
```

9. RECURSION

The calling function calls **Function Definition** repeatedly, but that **calling function** is also present in a **function definition** (only).

The calling function is repeated again and again by using a **calling function** that is present at the **function definition**, Whenever the function is called, then separate stack memory is allocated to the function at each and every function call.

For example, if you call a function 10 times using recursion then 10 separate stack memories are allocated. i.e. every function there should be a separate stack memory is allocated.

- Recursion is a bit difficult to understand. It is a good practice to terminate a recursion to avoid memory overload.

Syntax:

void fun_recurr();

```
void main()
{
//statements;
//calling function
fun_recurr();
}
//function definition/ called function
void fun_recurr()
{
//statements;
//calling function
fun_recurr();
}
```

Example 1:

An example program to print even numbers between 1 to 10 numbers using recursion.

Program:

```
#include <stdio.h>
void rec_even(int k);
void main()
{
int k=1;
rec_even(k);
}
void rec_even(int k)
{
if(k<=10)
{
if(k%2==0)
{
printf("%d is an even number\n", k);
}
rec_even(k+1);
}
}
```

Output:

2 is an even number
4 is an even number
6 is an even number
8 is an even number
10 is an even number

Explanation:

In the above problem

1. We ha ave calling function in the main () function it calls called function only once, i.e. rec_even(1)
2. We have function definition /called function this function contains another calling function rec_even (k+1). So, this function is called self call function or recursion function.
3. The above recursive function calls itself up to the base case value is reached. Once the base case value is reached the control returns to the previous calling function and after the control goes to previously calling function, then memory is deallocated in s,tock and the control return back up to calling functiothe n in main () function. Here the best case is if(k<=10), if this condition is true, then the recursion is stopped.

Pictorial Representation :

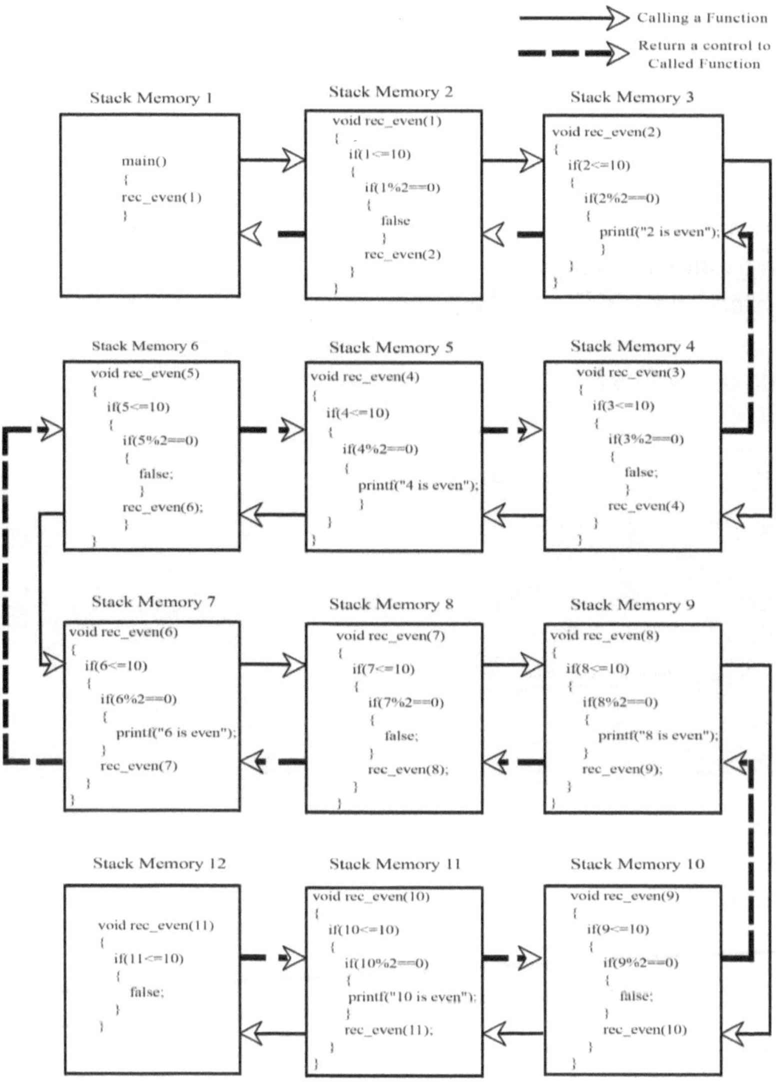

Figure 5.1 Pictorial Representation

Example 2:

An example program to print the sum of natural numbers using recursion.

Program:

```
#include <stdio.h>
int rec_sum(int);
void main()
[
int p, ret_value;
printf("Enter value_:");
scanf("%d\n", &p);
ret_value= rec_sum(p);
printf("Sum is %d", ret_value);
]
int rec_sum(int p)
[
if(p==1)
[
return 1;
]
else
[
return p+rec_sum(p-1);;
]
]
```

Output:

```
Enter value_: 4
Sum is 10
```

Pictorial Representation :

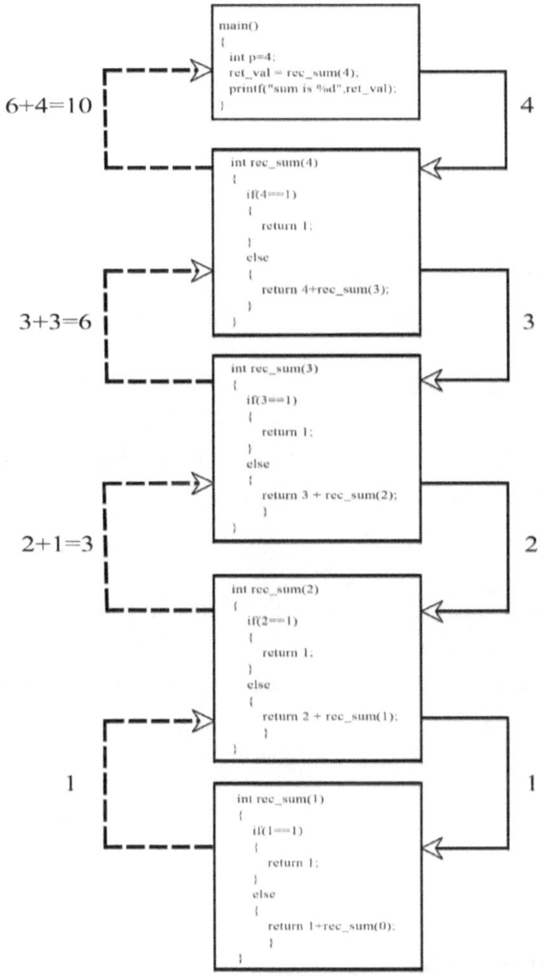

Figure 5.2 Pictorial Representation

Explanation:
In the above program

1. Calling function in the main() function calls called function with parameter value 4.
2. Here we have function definition / called function, this function contains another calling function, so this function becomes recursive function.

3. The above recursive function calls itself up to the base case value reached. Here base case condition is if(p==1). Once the base case value is reached the control returns the to previously calling function and after control the goes to the previously calling function, then memory is allocated in stock in control returns back up to the calling function in main ().

10. TEXT INPUT/OUTPUT

Introduction to Files :

A file is nothing but a data or sequence of bytes that can be stored in any external device-like a hard disk, pen drive, etc.

Basically, we have two types of files.

1. **Binary file** Binary files are the files that can store the data in the form of binary symbols (0's or 1's)
2. **Text file:** Text files are the files that can store the data in the form of ASCII or plain text.

Streams

1. The stream is nothing but a sequence of characters
2. Here input stream is the keyboard and the output stream is a console
3. The input and output performed with streams
4. Stream means a sequence of characters that are converted into lines and new line character
5. The C Standard library has many functions for taking Input and printing output

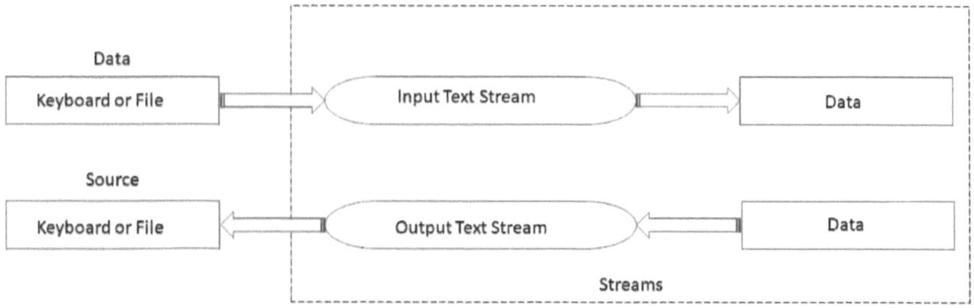

Figure 5.3 Text Input Output Streams

Above figure else but the input text stream read data from keyboard or file by using scanf( )or fscan()functions. The output text stream gets data by using printf( ) or a fprintf( ) to print data on a monitor or file.

Text Stream:

The text stream has alphabets, digits, and special characters by storing there ASCII values

Every New line terminated with a new line.'\n'

Stream File Processing:

If we want to use any file in the secondary storage device then we must create a stream.

There are four steps to processing a file.

1. Creating stream
2. Opening a file
3. Using the stream name
4. Closing the stream

1. Creating a Stream:

We create a stream by using file identifier

Example:

FILE * FP;

The file pointer (fp) is created to store the address of a file.

2. Opening a file :

The file function returns the address of a file which is stored in the stream pointer variable

fp = fopen("filename","mode");

3. Using the stream name :

Use stream pointer (fp) in all functions that need to access a particular file for input and output

4. Closing the stream :

When the use of the file is complete close file fclose(fp);

The system created streams :

Use standard stream names like printf( ) i.e, standard output stream i.e stdinCan f is a standard input stream that is

Deep streams are created by operating systems automatically

All the standard stream names are declared in stdio.h

No need to open or close the standard

Standard Library Input/Output Functions

Here we have many file handling functions that can perform operations on files.

File Modes :

While performing any operations like reading or writing on a file firstly, we need to open a file by using an open() function at the time of opening we need to mention mode of the file.

In case we mention 'r' (read mode) in open() function, the file will be opened in read mode.

In case we mention 'w' (write mode) in open() function, the file will be opened in write mode.

In case we mention 'a' (append mode) in open() function, the file will be opened in append mode.

Mode	Description
r	This is for to open a file in read mode only
w	This is for to open a file in write mode only
a	This is for to open a file in append mode
r+	This is nothing but read + write. This is same as "r" mode but using this you can modify the data but, this does not remove previous contents of a file
w+	This is nothing but write+read. This is same as "w" mode but it removes previous contents of a file
a+	This is nothing but append + read. This is same as "a" mode, but we can append data to the end of the file and we can read data from the file also

Table 5.1 File Modes

- **fopen()**:

This function is used to create a new file or open an already existing file in secondary storage device.

fopen() function works under #include<stdio.h> header file.

Syntax:

*file_ptr= fopen(filename, mode);

On success, fopen() returns address of starting character in a file.

On failure, fopen() returns NULL.

Here, *file_ptr means file pointer, filename means the name of the file or the path of file, and mode is read, write, or append mode.

Example:

int *file_ptr= fopen("abc.txt", "r");

Above file, abc.txt opens in read mode only.

int *file_ptr= fopen("abc.txt", "w");

Above file, abc.txt opens in write mode only.

int *file_ptr= fopen("abc.txt", "a");

Above file, abc.txt opens in append mode only.

fclose():

fclose() function is used to close the opened file system.

This function works under #include<stdio.h> header file.

Syntax:

fclose(file_pointer);

Example:

fclose(file_ptr);

On success, it returns 0.

On failure, it returns EOF.

getc():

This function is used to get a character from a file.

Syntax:

getc(file_pointer);

Example: getc(file_ptr);

putc():

putc() function works in two ways.

It is used to print a character on standard output(monitor).

Syntax:

putc(character);

Example: putc(ch_value);

// ch_value has character that is read from file

It is used to write character into a file.

Syntax:

putc(character, file_pointer);

Example:

putc(ch_value, file_ptr);

// here ch_value has character that is read from file.

// file_ptr means file pointer

Programs on Files

Program 1:

Design a C program to open a file. Write data into file, and close the file.

```
#include<stdio.h>
#include<stdlib.h>
void main()
{
```

```
char name[100];
// create file_pointer
FILE *file_ptr;
//open a file in write mode
file_ptr=fopen("abc.txt", "w");
if(file_ptr==NULL)
{
printf("Error while opening the file");
exit(0);
}
printf("Enter a name\n");
//read a string as input
getc(name);
//write the string into file
for(int p=0;name[p]!='\0';p++)
putc(name[p], file_ptr);
//closing a file_pointer
fclose(file_ptr);
printf("Data entered into abc.txt successfully");
}
```

Explanation:

1. Create a file pointer, i.e. FILE *file_ptr.
2. Next open a file in write "w" mode i.e. file_ptr=fopen("abc.txt", "w"). On success of above function fopen() returns the starting address to file_ptr. After that the file abc.txt allows to write data into that file. On failure of the above function, fopen() returns NULL value to file_ptr and prints "Error while opening the file" and exits from the program.
3. Declare a string char name[100] and initialize value to it using gets() function i.e.gets(name).
4. Read character by character from string and write every character into a file using putc() function i.e.putc(name[p], file_ptr).

Above putc() function puts character by character into file_ptr stream.

After completion of writing into file, it is good practice to close opened file using fclose() function i.e. fclose(file_ptr)

Input:

Enter a name

Koti Mani Kumar

Output:

Data entered into abc.txt successfully.

After execution, a file "abc.txt" is created in the same directory where the program is saved.

Program 2:

Design a C program to open a file, read data from a file and print it on screen.

```
#include<stdio.h>
#include<stdlib.h>
void main()
{
//create a file pointer
FILE *file_ptr;
char ch_val;
//open a file in read mode
file_ptr=fopen("abc.txt", "r");
if(file_ptr==NULL)
{
printf("Error while opening the file");
exit (0);
}
printf("Data in abc.txt is: \n");
while((ch_val=getc(file_ptr))!=EOF)
{
printf("%c", ch_val);
}
fclose(file_ptr);
}
```

Explanation:

In the above program,

1. Create a file pointer, i.e. FILE *file_ptr.
2. Next open a file in read "r" mode i.e. file_ptr=fopen("abc.txt", "r"). On the success of the above function fopen() returns the starting address to

file_ptr. After that, the file abc.txt allows writing data into that file. On failure of the above function, fopen() returns NULL value to file_ptr and prints “Error while opening the file” and exits from the program.

3. Next statement prints “Data in abc.txt is:”
4. Next statement is in while loop, iterates up to end of the file i.e. EOF and prints character by character on monitor.Here we use getc() function to get character by character from abc.txt file and stores it in ch_val variable and the value present in ch_value is printed on the screen.
5. After completion of writing into file, it is good practice to close opened file using fclose() function i.e.fclose(file_ptr)

“abc.txt” contains the text:

Koti Mani Kumar

On execution of the above function, the output is displayed as:

Data in abc.txt is:

Koti Mani Kumar

Program 3:

Design a C program to copy one file to another

```
#include<stdio.h>
#include<stdlib.h>
void main()
{
char ch_val;
//create file pointers
FILE *file_ptr1, *file_ptr2;
//open file in read mode to read read data from that file
file_ptr1=fopen("abc.txt", "r");
//open file in write mode to write data
file_ptr2=fopen("xyz.txt", "w");
if(file_ptr1==NULL || file_ptr2==NULL)
{
printf("Error while opening the file");
exit(0);
}
// copy the data from abc.txt to xyz.tx
while((ch_val=getc(file_ptr1))!=EOF)
putc(ch_val, file_ptr2);
```

```
fclose(file_ptr1);
fclose(file_ptr2);
printf("Data entered from abc.txt to xyz.txt successfully");
}
```

Output:

Data entered from abc.txt to xyz.txt successfully

Explanation:

In the above program

1. Create two file pointers i.e. FILE *file_ptr1, *file_fptr2.
2. Open abc.txt file in read mode to read data from that file using fopen("abc.txt", "r") and also open xyz.txt in write mode to write data into it using fopen("xyz.txt", "w")
3. Check if both the files are opened or not using if condition i.e.

if(file_ptr1==NULL || file_ptr2==NULL)

If either of the file pointers returns NULL value, error message is displayed and the program is terminated. Otherwise the process continues.

1. Copy the data from "abc.txt" to "xyz.txt" character by character using getc() and putc() as input and output functions respectively.
2. After the copying is done successfully, a message "Data entered from abc.txt to xyz.txt successfully" is printed

Data in the file "abc.txt" is:

Koti Mani Kumar

After execution, the data in "xyz.txt" is:

Koti Mani Kumar

Program 4:

Design a C program to merge two files

```
#include<stdio.h>
#include<stdlib.h>
void main()
{
char ch_val;
//create file pointers
FILE *file_ptr1, *file_ptr2, *file_ptr3;
```

```
//open abc.txt and xyz.txt in read mode
file_ptr1=fopen("abc.txt", "r");
file_ptr2=fopen("xyz.txt", "r");
//open uvw.txt in write mode
file_ptr3=fopen("uvw.txt", "w");
if(file_ptr1==NULL || file_ptr2==NULL|| file_ptr3==NULL)
{
printf("Error while opening the file");
exit(0);
}
//copy data from abc.txt to uvw.txt
while((ch_val=getc(file_ptr1))!=EOF)
putc(ch_val, file_ptr3);
putc('\t', file_ptr3);
//copy data from xyz.txt to uvw.txt
while((ch_val=getc(file_ptr2))!=EOF)
putc(ch_val, file_ptr3);
printf("Two files merged into uvw.txt successfully");
fclose(file_ptr1);
fclose(file_ptr2);
fclose(file_ptr3);
}
```

Output:

Two files merged into uvw.txt successfully

Explanation:

In the above program

1. Create file pointers i.e. FILE *file_ptr1, *file_ptr2, *file_ptr3.
2. Open abc.txt and xyz.txt in read mode to read data from these two files and open uvw.txt file in write mode to write data into it.
3. Check if all the three files are open or not using the "if" condition.If at least one of the files is not opened successfully, then the program is terminated.
4. Copy the data from "abc.txt" to "uvw.txt" character by character using getc() and putc() function for read and write operations respectively.putc('\t', file_ptr3) is used to put space after completing reading text from "abc.txt"

5. Now, copy the data from "xyz.txt" to "uvw.txt" character by character using getc() and putc() function for read and write operations respectively.
6. After copying both the files into "uvw.txt" print "Two files merged into uvw.txt successfully" on screen.
7. Close the three files i.e. fclose(file_ptr1); fclose(file_ptr2); fclose(file_ptr3);

Output :

Let the file "abc.txt" contains the text:

Koti Mani Kumar

Let the file "xyz.txt" contains the text:

Department of CSE

After the execution of above program, the function "uvw.txt" contains the text:

Koti Mani Kumar Department of CSE

Formatting input/output function:

The C stdio.h library have 2 general functions

1. fscanf( )
2. fprintf( )

Above two functions are used with any text stream.

fscanf( ):

It is used to read the data from a text file. It returns EOF data from a text file.

Syntax:

fscanf(fp,"format list",address list)

Example:

Fscanf(fp,"%s",variable_name);

fprintf( ):

It is used to write the data into the file.

Syntax:

fprintf("file_pointer","format list",variable_list);

Example:

```
fprintf(fp,"%d \n ",roll_no);
```

Example program on Formatting input/output function:

```
#include<stdio.h>
#include<string.h>
#include<stdlib.h>
int main()
{
FILE * fp;
int emp_id;
char emp_name[100];
char buff[100];
float sal;
fp = fopen("emp.txt","w");
if(fp == NULL)
{
perror("Error in creating or opening a file");
exit(0);
}
emp_id = 1248;
strcpy(emp_name , "Manasa");
sal = 2400;
//Write the data into the file.
fprintf(fp,"Employee id = %d \n",emp_id);
fprintf(fp,"Employee name = %s \n",emp_name);
fprintf(fp,"Employee salary = %f \n",sal);
fclose(fp);
//Read the data from a file
fp = fopen("emp.txt","r");
while((fscanf(fp,"%s",buff)) != EOF)
{
printf("%s \n", buff);
}
fclose(fp);
return 0 ;
}
```

Output:

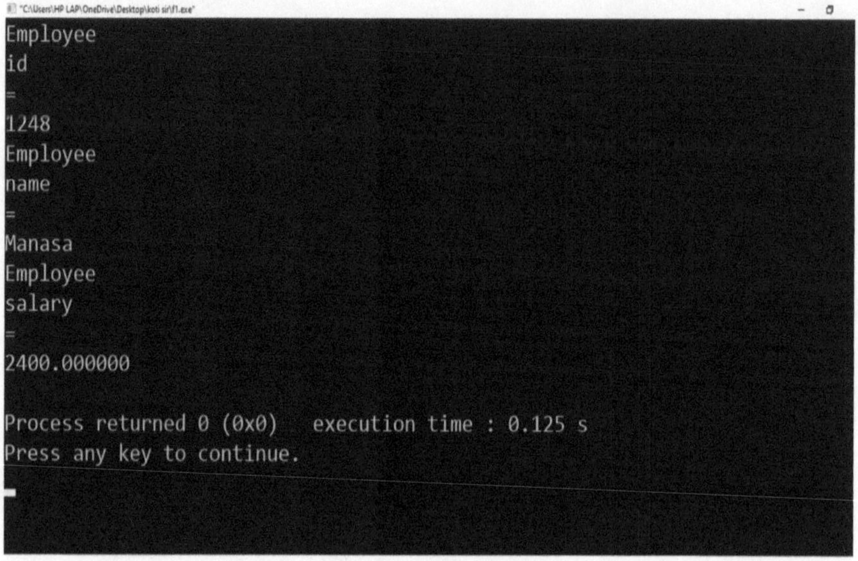
"C:\Users\HP LAP\OneDrive\Desktop\koti sir\f1.exe"
Employee
id
=
1248
Employee
name
=
Manasa
Employee
salary
=
2400.000000
Process returned 0 (0x0)   execution time : 0.125 s
Press any key to continue.

Figure 5.4

Character Input/Output:

The character input function reads only one character at a line from the text stream.

We use fget( ) function to read data character from text stream.

fget( ) returns the present position of a character.

Syntax:

fget(file_pointer);

Example:

char ch;

ch = fget(fp);

The character output function writes only one character at a time to a text stream.

We use the fputc( ) function to print the data character by character to a text stream.

Syntax:

fputc(variable,file_pointer);

Example:

fputc('d',fp);B

11. BINARY INPUT/OUTPUT FUNCTIONS

Text versus Binary Streams

Text Stream :

The text stream has alphabets, digits, and special characters

Every New line terminated with a new line.'\n'

How to store 549A in a Text file

Firstly, we convert 5 into ASCII value then, convert that ASCII value into its relevant binary and same for 4 and 9 . Then,we should convert A to its ASCII value and convert into to its relevant Binary value.

ASCII value of **5** is 53

ASCII value of **4** is 52

ASCII value of **9** is 57

ASCII value of **A** is 65

5	4	9	A
00110101	00110100	00111001	01000001

Figure 5.4 storing 549A in a Text file

Binary Streams :

A binary file is a file that stores the data in the form of a computer's internal format

A binary file is a sequence of collection of B which is not in the human-understandable language

How to store 549A in a binary file

549		A
00000010	00100101	01000001

Figure 5.5 storing 549A in a binary file

Standard library function for files :

1. Block Input or output functions

In C language block input is used to read data from binary files and block output is used to write data to binary files

Block read function is used to read the data by using the file read function from the binary file

Syntax:

fread(&structure variable,sizeof(structure variable)No.of structure variables,file pointer);

Example:

fread(&s,sizeof(s),1,fp)

Block right function is used to write the data by using file write to a binary file

Syntax:

fwrite(&structure variable,sizeof(structure variable),No.of Structure variables,file pointer);

Example:

fwrite(&s,sizeof(s),1,fp);

Example program to illustrate fwrite( )

```
#include <stdio.h>
    #include <string.h>
    #include <stdlib.h>
    struct Employee {
    int empid;
    char ename[50];
    float sal;
    };
    int main()
    {
    struct Employee e;
    FILE *fp;
    fp = fopen("binaryfile.txt", "wb");
```

```
printf("Enter Employee id: ");
scanf("%d", &e.empid);
printf("Enter Employee Name: ");
scanf("%s", e.ename);
printf("Enter Salary: ");
scanf("%f", &e.sal);
fwrite(&e, sizeof(e), 1, fp);
fclose(fp);
return 0;
}
```

Output :

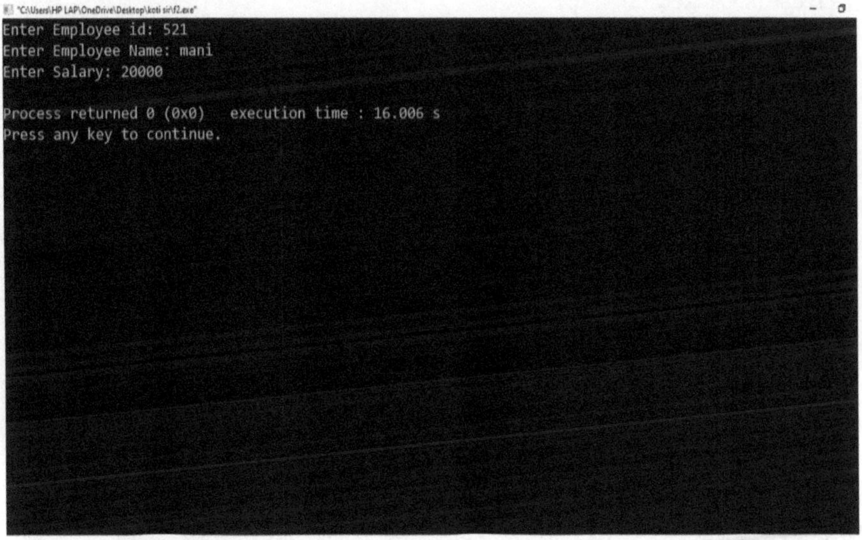

Enter Employee id: 521
Enter Employee Name: mani
Enter Salary: 20000
Process returned 0 (0x0)   execution time : 16.006 s
Press any key to continue.

Explanation :

In the above program, fwrite function is used to write data in file pointer fp.

&e means the address of the structure variable

The size of(e) means the size of the structure.

1(one) means a total number of records or variable fp is a file pointer that can store the above data.

Example program to illustrate fread function.

```
#include <stdio.h>
```

```
#include <stdlib.h>
struct Employee
{
int empid;
char sname[20];
float sal;
};
int main()
{
struct Employee e;
FILE *fp;
fp = fopen("binaryfile.txt", "rb");
fread(&e, sizeof(e), 1, fp);
printf("%d, %s, %f", e.empid, e.sname, e.sal);
return 0;
}
```

Output :

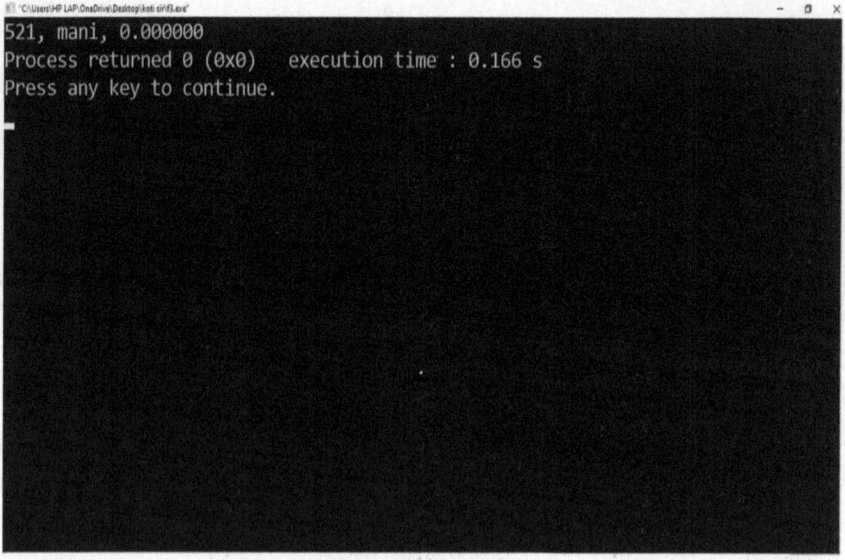

521, mani, 0.000000
Process returned 0 (0x0)   execution time : 0.166 s
Press any key to continue.

Output :

In the above program fread function is used to read data from binary file pointer fp.

&e address of structure variable

Same as above

2. Status function feof( ) ,ferrors,clear err( ) :

***feof( ):**

It is used to identify whether the control reaches the end of the file or not

Syntax:

Int feof(file pointer);

If feof a true value that means the end of the file reached otherwise false

***ferror( ):**

It is used to check/ identify the error status of a file.

If the ferror function returns 0 error has occurred otherwise error occurred.

Syntax:

int ferror(file pointer);

***clearer( ) :**

Is used to reset the error status of a file.

Syntax:

Void clear err(file pointer)

3. Positionery functions rewind ( ), ftell ( ) , fseek ( ):

rewind ( ):

The use of rewind( ) in the function is to set the cursor to the beginning of the file from anywhere in the file.

Syntax:

Void rewind(file pointer);

Example:

```
#include<stdio.h>
#include<stdlib.h>
int main()
{
FILE * fp;
char ch;
fp = fopen("abc.txt","r");
while(!feof(fp))
{
ch = fgetc(fp);
printf("%c",ch);
```

```
}
//File pointer reaches to end of the file rewind(fp);
//This brings the file pointr to beginning
while(!feof(fp))
{
ch = fgetc(fp);
printf("%c",ch);
}
fclose(fp);
return 0;
}
```

Output:

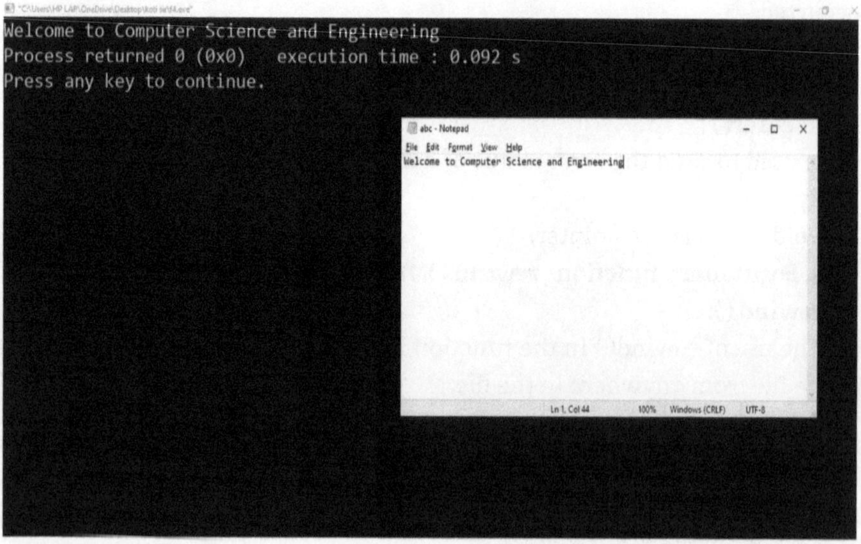

ftell( ):

This is used to tell current position of the file pointer

Syntax:

longint ftell(file_pointer);

Example :

```
#include<stdio.h>
int main()
{
```

```
FILE * fp;
int position;
fp = fopen ("abc.txt","r");
position = ftell(fp);
printf("%d",position);
fseek(fp,5,SEEK_SET);
printf("%d",ftell(fp));
fclose(fp);
return 0;
}
```

Output :

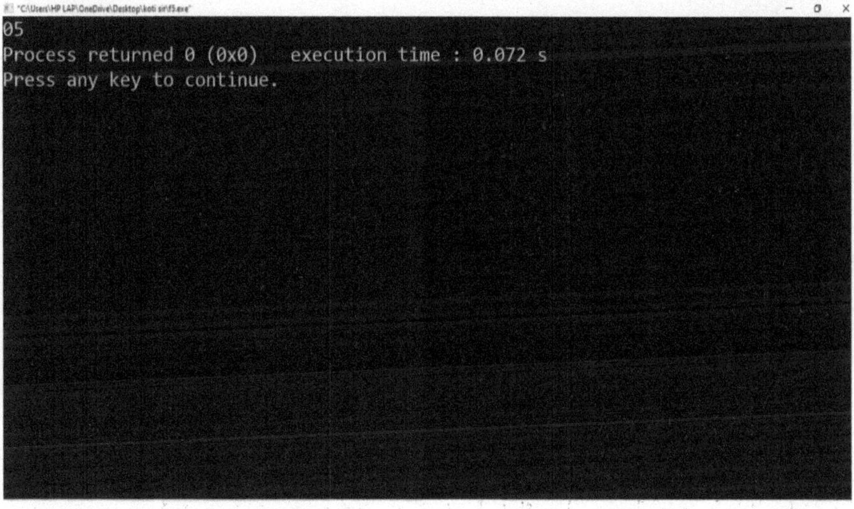

fseek( ):

Use it to allow to place the file pointer at any desired position.

Syntax :

fseek(file_pointer,offset,position);

*File pointer means file stream

*Offset means how many characters are to be moved. After value may be positive or negative

A positive offset value means the more specified number of characters toward the forward direction

A negative offset value means the more specified number of characters in the forward-backward direction.

Position value may be either 0 or 1 or 2.

0 specifies that beginning of the file

1 specifies that the current position of the file

2 specifies the end of the file.

position means from which position we are going to add offset.

Here we have three values

1.SEEK_SET beginning of the file

2. SEEK_ CUR current position of the file

3.SEEK_END end of the file

Example:

```
#include<stdio.h>
int main()
{
FILE * fp;
char ch;
fp = fopen("abc.txt","r");
if(fp == NULL)
{
printf("Error in opening a file");
exit(0);
}
fseek(fp,6,SEEK_SET);//Cursor sets after 6th character
ch = fgetc(fp);
printf("%c",ch);
//Cursor moves 4 bytes towards backward direction from current position
fseek(fp,4,SEEK_CUR);
ch = fgetc(fp);
printf("%c",ch);
//From the end move 4 btes towards backward direction
fseek(fp,-4,SEEK_END);
ch = fgetc(fp);
printf("%c",ch);
fclose(fp);
return 0;
}
```

Output :

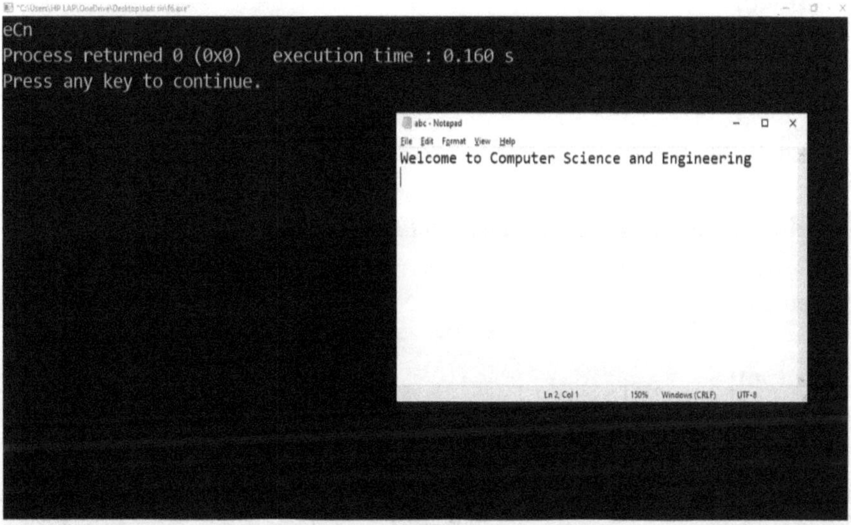

4. System File operations :

The System file operations are remove( ) ,rename( ) and tempfile( ).

remove( ):

Remove this function is used to remove or delete the file

Syntax:

int remove(filename);

Parameters:

The remove function returns 0 on successfully deleted or remover otherwise returns -1 an error.

Example :

```
#include<stdio.h>
int main()
{
int r;
FILE *fp;
fp=fopen("abc.txt","W");
```

```
fprintf(fp,"%s","c programming");
r = remove("abc.txt");
if(r==0)
{
printf("file deleted/removed successfully");
}
else
{
printf("error occurred in deleting a file");
}
return 0;
}
```

Output:

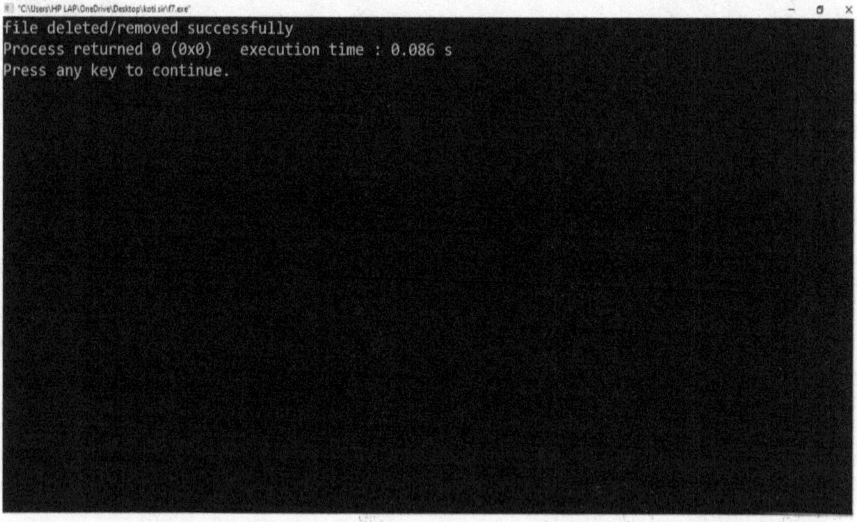

rename( ):

This function is used to rename the file. It works under stdio.h header file.

Syntax:

int remove(old filename,newfilename);

Example :

```
#include<stdio.h>
```

```
int main()
{
int r_name = rename("abc.txt", "def.txt");
if(r_name == 0)
{
printf("The file is renamed to def.txt");
}
else
{
printf("Error occurred in remaining a file");
}
return 0;
}
```

Output:

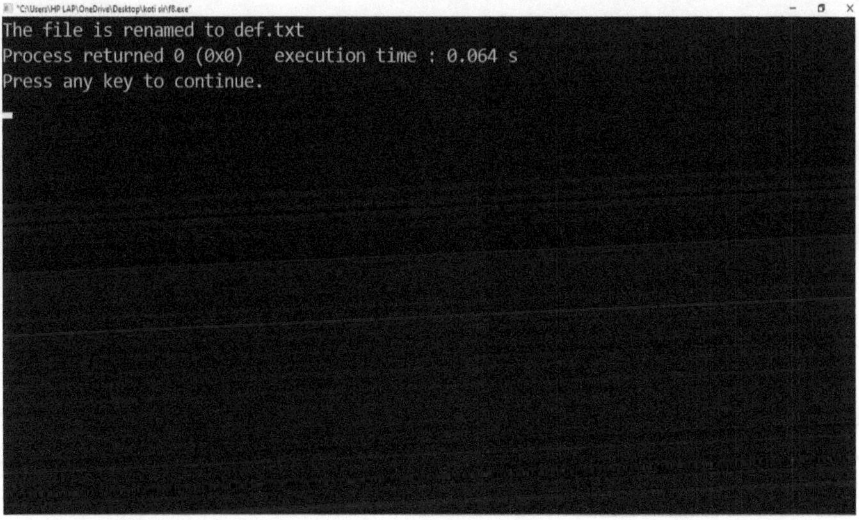
The file is renamed to def.txt
Process returned 0 (0x0)   execution time : 0.064 s
Press any key to continue.

tempfile( ):

Whenever the tempfile( ) function is executed then the temporary file is created and automatically deleted.

Whenever the fclose ( ) function gets executed for program terminates.

Syntax:

FILE * tempfile(void)

Example :

```
#include <stdio.h>
int main()
{
char c[] = "T. Koti Mani Kumar";
int i = 0;
FILE* fp = tmpfile(); //make the file pointer as temporary file.
fp = fopen("file.txt", "w");
if (fp == NULL)
{
puts("Error in creating temporary file");
return 0;
}
puts("Temporary file created successfully");
while (c[i] != '\0')
{
fputc(c[i], fp);
i++;
}
fclose(fp);
fp = fopen("file.txt", "r");
rewind(fp); //set the pointer at the beginning of the stream of the file pointer.
while (!feof(fp))
putchar(fgetc(fp));
fclose(fp); //closing the file pointer
}
```

Output :

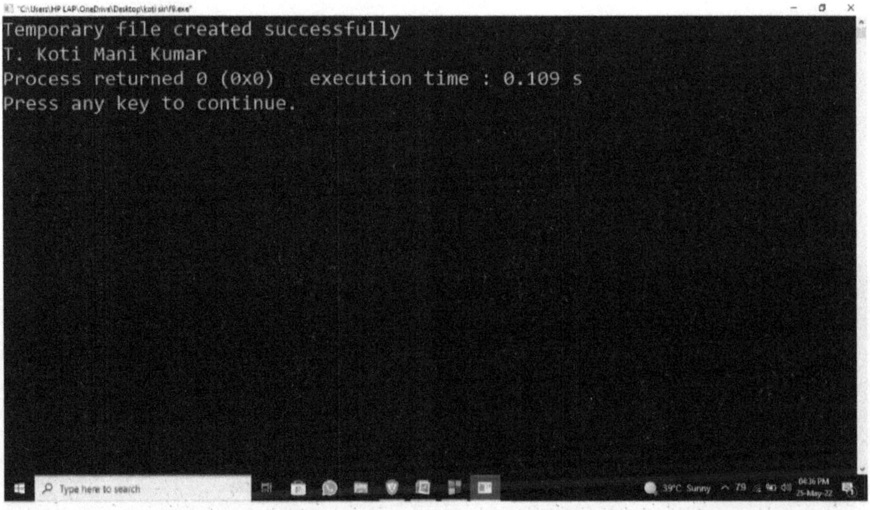
Temporary file created successfully
T. Koti Mani Kumar
Process returned 0 (0x0)   execution time : 0.109 s
Press any key to continue.
Type here to search

ABOUT THE AUTHOR

T. N. S. Koti Mani Kumar

Mr. **T. N. S. Koti Mani Kumar** completed his **B.Tech** in Information Technology and **M.Tech** in Computer Science and Engineering.He is pursuing a **Ph.D.** in CSE from Bharath University, Tamilnadu. He was appointed as **Assistant Professor** in the **Department of Computer Science and Engineering at Sir C R Reddy College of Engineering**, Eluru, West Godavari district, Andhra Pradesh.

He is Microsoft certified in Microsoft Dynamics CRM 2016 customization and configuration (Candidate ID: Ms061 5248291). He has 2+ years of industrial experience with NET technologies using ASP.NET, C# NET, WCF, and MS SQL server 2008 & 2012. He has 5+ years of experience in teaching. His area of interest is in C, Java, Python, Computer Networks and Machine Learning.

www.ingramcontent.com/pod-product-compliance
Lightning Source LLC
Chambersburg PA
CBHW051214130726
47988CB00001B/95
* 9 7 9 8 8 8 7 1 7 5 9 6 6 *